# DEAREST CASEY

J. P. Beuther

Copyright © 2012 J. P. Beuther
All rights reserved.
ISBN: : 1478338334
ISBN 13: 9781478338338

# TABLE OF CONTENTS

| | | |
|---|---|---|
| CHAPTER 1 | SCHOOL'S BACK | 1 |
| CHAPTER 2 | THE NEW GIRL | 3 |
| CHAPTER 3 | ASHLEIGH'S VISIT | 9 |
| CHAPTER 4 | POETRY PROJECT PRESENTATION DAY | 15 |
| CHAPTER 5 | THE FIRST GAME | 19 |
| CHAPTER 6 | CASEY'S FIRST VARSITY PRACTICE | 23 |
| CHAPTER 7 | ASHLEIGH'S BIRTHDAY | 27 |
| CHAPTER 8 | THE HIKE | 31 |
| CHAPTER 9 | CHEROKEE VS. WEST FINALS | 37 |
| CHAPTER 10 | ROLLER SKATING | 43 |
| CHAPTER 11 | CASEY & ASHLEIGH'S SECOND ENGLISH PROJECT | 47 |
| CHAPTER 12 | ASHLEIGH AND CASEY'S PRESENTATION | 53 |
| CHAPTER 13 | MR. RYAN'S TALK | 57 |
| CHAPTER 14 | CASEY AND ASHLEIGH GO TO THE MOVIES | 61 |

| CHAPTER 15 | ASHLEIGH AND CASEY'S FILM PRESENTATION ..................... 67 |
|---|---|
| CHAPTER 16 | CASEY'S MEETING WITH DR. WANG ................... 73 |
| CHAPTER 17 | CASEY AND ASHLEIGH'S BOWLING DATE ..................... 79 |
| CHAPTER 18 | CASEY'S FIRST DATE ............ 83 |
| CHAPTER 19 | ACADEMIC AWARD CEREMONY ........................... 89 |
| CHAPTER 20 | SOCCER CAMP ..................... 93 |
| CHAPTER 21 | THE REMATCH - WEST VS. CHEROKEE'S ........ 99 |
| CHAPTER 22 | THE CELEBRATION .............. 123 |

It occurs during Casey Winter's
darkest hour, during her moment of need, the
greatest miracle life has to offer,
the gift of friendship.

Dedicated to my
"SWEET BABY JAMES"
you are my "HEART"
My life will never be the same.
We never did get that dance
that you promised me. We dance
every night in my dreams!

CHERISH

*The life given us by nature is short but
the memory of a well spent life is eternal.-Cicero*

A Special thank you to Jane Travers,
and her English Dept. at Udall Middle School,
West Islip, NY.  Her letter gave me the courage to
publish Jim's manuscript.

⌘ ⌘ ⌘

*If I can stop one heart from breaking,*
*I shall not live in vain;*
*If I can ease one life the aching,*
*Or cool one pain,*
*Or help one fainting robin*
*Unto his nest again,*
*I shall not live in vain.*

*Emily Dickinson*

I want to thank Jim's family friends and colleagues for their caring and support. A very special thank you to Brendan Cawley for not only being a loyal friend but being Jim's "Brother." Matt Murphy and John Kennedy for standing by Jim through not only the good times but the bad. I want to thank Al for being my rock and a true friend and surrogate Dad to James. For His step dad the late John Loch for instilling in James not only the importance of family values, but pride in himself his faith and respect for others. His sister Donna for being his second Mama! His brother George, his sister Kerri, and his girlfriend Kelly for just loving him without judgement. My sister Vivie for being just a text away, and my old friend Virginia and new friend Pat for being just a phone call away whenever I needed them.

I cannot leave out my dear cousin Joan, Jim's God Mom and His Aunt Carol and Uncle John for standing close by my side and getting me through one of the darkest times of my life. I will never forget that. And last but not least to all his students that he loved so much. He never had the time to

## DEAREST CASEY

have any of his own, but each and every one of you were his.  And most of all his Soccer teams, past and present.  I would  get phone calls and run downs after every game.  He was so passionate about HIS GIRLS!  Love to you all for loving him!

# Chapter 1

## SCHOOLS BACK

Preparing for the first day of school, Casey found herself feeling sad. The recent NEWS of her mother's illness had shattered her heart into a million pieces. Casey, gazing into the mirror as she got ready for school, began to reflect on her emotions at the very moment she learned of the news back in July:

CASEY, THIS CAN'T BE REAL! WHY DOES MOM HAVE TO BE SICK? I AM ONLY THIRTEEN... THIS CAN'T BE REAL...CASEY, THIS ISN'T REALLY HAPPENING... THERE IS JUST NO WAY...

Snapping out of her flashback, Casey gazed upon the photo. It was her favorite picture! It was taken when Casey was six years old. In the picture, the two of them are laughing. Of course, Casey's dad had taken the picture. He was always certain to capture the family's memories to share with all, especially the three of them: Casey, Mom and Dad.

## DEAREST CASEY

The day of the picture was an important day. It was Casey's very first soccer game, and Mom was the team's coach. In the photo, Casey is dressed warm to protect her from the brisk New York autumn air. Yet again, the photo stirred Casey's emotions:

MOM ALWAYS PROTECTED ME FROM THE COLD. SHE ALWAYS DRESSED ME FOR SOCCER AND SCHOOL WHEN I WAS LITTLE. MOM, HOW, AM I GOING TO LIVE WITHOUT YOU?

Snapping back again to reality, Casey took a deep breath to compose herself before going downstairs for breakfast.

OKAY CASEY, PUT ON YOUR HAPPY MASK… DON'T LET MOM AND DAD SEE YOU UPSET. CASEY, ALL SMILES THIS MORNING …CASEY, REMEMBER, IT IS THE FIRST DAY OF SCHOOL. MOM AND DAD KNOW HOW MUCH YOU LOVE PLAYING FOR THE SCHOOL SOCCER TEAM, AND TODAY IS THE FIRST DAY OF PRACTICE.

"Casey, come down for breakfast! It's getting late," bellowed Mrs. Winter.

OKAY CASEY, HERE WE GO - THE FIRST DAY OF EIGHTH GRADE…

## Chapter 2

# THE NEW GIRL

"Hello, young lady. The sixth grade classrooms are on the first floor," spoke Mr. Ryan. The tiny girl with big round glasses smiled and responded: "I am in the eighth grade sir." The new girl's confident, spry response brought and instantaneous smile to Casey's face.

"Why I apologize! Is this your first day at West Middle School?" Mr. Ryan, Casey's English teacher and the girl's soccer coach, smiled at the sight of the new girl. Although she appeared much younger than her age, the manner in which she spoke and carried herself seemed to be that of an eighth grader.

"What is your name?"

"Ashleigh Marino sir."

"Why Ashleigh, it is a pleasure to have you with us."

"Thank you sir."

As the new girl looked for a seat, Casey recognized that the seat next to her was available.

"Hey Ashleigh, would you like to sit next to me" offered Casey?  "Why sure" Ashleigh excitedly responded in a squeaky voice.

As Mr. Ryan discussed the guideline and rules for English class, Casey glanced over at the new girl Ashleigh.  Ashleigh was so tiny that her legs angled above the classroom floor, not long enough to reach the tiles.  However, it was Ashleigh's smile and confidence that intrigued Casey.  Casey felt a strong connection with the new girl.  Casey admired how happy Ashleigh was.  Casey admired her huge smile and confidence:

She is so small, but she is so confident; She is happy!  I would like to be as happy as Ashleigh, pondered Casey.

"Class, to begin the school year, we are going to construct a poetry project".

Upon hearing Mr. Ryan's words, a few audible sighs and grumbles filled the room.  "That is what I expected; however, we must learn to appreciate the beautiful genre of poetry."  "How"? Shouted a boy from the back of the class.  "I will address your question," was Mr Ryan's confident response.

# THE NEW GIRL

"Class, poetry has the power to turn despair into joy. Poetry can turn death into life poetry can turn a rainy day sunny poetry can turn hate into love..."

As usual, Mr. Ryan's words excited the class. He was Casey's favorite teacher. She liked all her teacher's, but Mr. Ryan seemed to spark creativity that Casey never thought she possessed. The students loved his group projects. Also, Mr. Ryan was a really good soccer coach. West Middle School had been undefeated three years in a row with Mr. Ryan as coach. As with English class, Mr. Ryan made soccer practice fun.

"In addition, you will create your poetry project with a partner. I would rather not be in charge of pairing you up. I believe you are mature enough to select your own partners," instructed Mr. Ryan.

"Casey, would you like to be my partner?" squeaked Ashleigh. "I would love to be your partner" Casey cheerfully responded. The new girl seemed to make Casey's hidden depression subside. Casey found herself thinking:

HEY CASEY MAYBE MR. RYAN IS ONTO SOMETHING - PERHAPS DESPAIR CAN BE TURNED INTO JOY!

"Casey here is my phone number" Ashleigh continued to neatly write in Casey's agenda book. "Casey, why don't you call me tonight so we can begin to go over ideas for the project." "Sounds great Ashleigh, but I can't call you until 7:30. I have soccer practice after school, and after practice I do my homework and eat dinner." Ashleigh's expression was one of excitement: "I love soccer. My older sister plays on the school team too. She is a freshman and she made the Varsity team." "Do you play Soccer?" Casey asked. "No, I like to watch. I played last year, but I got hurt too often; my parents want me to wait a year before I try again. As you can see Casey I am a bit small for my age." "Maybe you can be our team manager? Mr. Ryan is the coach he seems to really like you already... We should ask him?" "Right on Casey, that sounds righteous! I am totally stoked!" Ashleigh replied.

"Where are you from Ashleigh? You got a cool accent, it is different from how people talk in New York?" "I am from Seattle, Washington. My father is a pilot for Northwestern Airlines. We moved here because it will help my Dad spend more time with us. I don't know why moving here will help him do that, but it seems like a good reason. My

Dad is great and so is my Mother. They are so much fun..." Then Ashleigh made Casey laugh hysterically by putting on her version of the New York accent: "Hey Casey, New York is like the bomb! Yo!"

As the new friends walked down the hallway together, Casey discovered herself happy. The depression that haunted her SINCE THE NEWS had subsided. "Wow! Your sister made varsity as a freshman? She must be awesome," inquired Casey. "Yeah, she is really good She is small too, but she is really fast. I hope I can play like her someday?" was Ashleigh's response.

For the very first time since they met, Casey recognized a hint of hidden sadness within Ashleigh, especially recognizing that huge smile momentarily subside. "Sure you will, Ashleigh...you will play soccer again." "I hope so Casey. I really hope so."

The first day of practice went well for Casey. She was excited to be on the field again, especially after such a boring depressing summer. Casey, while playing soccer always felt happy. Playing the game she loved, Casey only focused on soccer the game the practice the moment she had the ball at her feet the instant in which she would decide to pass, dribble or shoot!  After practice Casey felt invigorated.  However, her walk home grew glum as she pondered THE NEWS.

CANCER, WHY DO PEOPLE GET CANCER? CAN CANCER BE CURED?  WHY DOES MOM HAVE TO HAVE CANCER NOW? WHY ARE THEY TELLING ME IT IS ALMOST IMPOSSIBLE FOR MOM TO SURVIVE?  NOTHING IS IMPOSSIBLE...

The cancer thoughts clouded Casey's mind like an incoming thunder storm.  The ten minute walk home gave Casey time to really reflect on her mother's illness.  The walk home allowed her time to clear her mind before facing her parents.  Casey knew how much it upset her parents to see her unhappy.  Although she was unhappy on the inside, Casey became good at wearing the happy mask in front of her parents.

OKAY CASEY, PUT ON YOUR HAPPY MASK... THOUGHT CASEY AS SHE OPENED THE DOOR TO HER HOUSE.

## Chapter 3

# ASHLEIGH'S VISIT

It was on the first Saturday of the new school year that Ashley visited Casey's home for the first time. "Why hello, you must be Ashleigh. Casey has been telling us all about you this week," spoke Mrs. Winter. "Hello Mrs. Winter, it is a pleasure to meet you.

Sadly before Ashleigh arrived, Casey was crying in secret in her room. Her parents told her that Mom's cancer had spread. Then they told her about the hospital - Mom would be going to the hospital for, as Dad said: "An extended stay..."The discussion occurred at the breakfast table. Before Ashleigh's visit, Casey had all morning to reflect upon the tragic news.

IT'S ALL COMING TO AN END THE DREAMS THE TWO OF THEM HAD ABOUT THE FUTURE.

Gazing down at the picture on her dresser beside the mirror, Casey saw the image. While staring at the portrait, Casey began to think about the exact day the picture was taken. Although it was a long time ago, she remembered the day perfectly.

IT WAS MY FIRST SOCCER GAME, AND MOM WAS THE COACH. WE LOST FIVE OR SIX TO NOTHING, BUT MOM BOUGHT ALL THE GIRLS ON THE TEAM SODAS FROM THE VENDOR. I THINK I GOT A CHERRY COLA-YES, I GOT A CHERRY COLA - I REMEMBER.

Casey could remember Mom's words on the car ride home after the first game. "My dearest Casey, you played so well. "You almost scored two goals. It was all my fault! I did not tie your laces tight enough, and that is the reason you tripped before you shot the ball on the breakaway..."Mommy, don't be silly! I tripped on my own. I got excited when I thought I was going to score my first goal...I tripped on my own!" Casey then remembered the giggling and her mother gently touching her cheek. Then her memory was abruptly interrupted by the sound of her mother's voice.

"Casey, Ashleigh is here." Casey gathered herself, quickly wiping her face clean of tears. Lately Casey had become adept at changing masks. Okay Casey off with the sad mask. It's time to be happy Casey. Besides you adore Ashleigh.

"Hi Ashleigh, what would you like to do today?" asked Casey. "Would you like to go horse back riding?" "Wow, that sounds great!" Casey enthusiastically responded.

She always wanted to ride a horse. She seemed to never get the chance, or make the chance. Casey confidently asked:

"Mom, may I go horseback riding..."

Before Casey could finish the question, her mother responded:

"Absolutely! Do you girls need some money?"

It seemed as though Ashleigh had the moment rehearsed.

"Mrs. Winter, my parents gave me money. It doesn't cost much, and then after you get the lesson you may ride the horse for another half hour. It is very safe. You are not allowed to ride the trails till after the fifth lesson. The beginners ride in a ring around the stable. As far as a ride is concerned, the stable is less then two miles away, we can walk, it's such a beautiful day."

Casey and Ashleigh loved how beautiful the horses were: "Ashleigh just smiled from ear to ear the entire day at the stable...She must be the happiest girl in the world thought Casey to herself often throughout the day.

# DEAREST CASEY

To Casey's surprise, it seemed as though Ashleigh's emotions would become her own emotions as well. Casey's smile laughter and joy was no longer a mask. She didn't need the mask now as long as she was with Ashleigh.

Ashleigh seemed much different from her soccer friends. Ashleigh was spontaneous. Casey knew she would not have gone horseback riding with her other friends, and she definitely would not have walked two miles to get to the stables, and then back home again! Casey loved the walking…they took huge breaths during the walk to and from the horse stable.

As Casey and Ashleigh walked home, they spoke about the horses. Next, they spoke about the lesson and how much they learned from the instructor. Then they talked about the different shapes of the clouds, and how warm the sun felt.

Ashleigh, living only minutes from Casey's house, declined Casey's offer to come inside her house. "I need to get home. I have to walk my dog. He needs and hour of exercise every day. Then I need to do my reading homework for Mr. Ryan." I will come over tomorrow so we can talk about ideas for next Friday's poetry project.

# ASHLEIGH'S VISIT

Over the course of a few hours much laughter and conversation flowed and so did their new found friendship.

## Chapter 4

# POETRY PROJECT PRESENTATION DAY

Casey and Ashleigh devoted hours of tireless effort into creating their poetry project. The night before it was due, they met at the town library to put "the finishing touches on it." As Ashleigh would say!

It seemed at least from Casey's perspective, that Ashleigh was the more creative out of the two of them. However, Casey deftly organized the poems as well as typed them out on her computer. As Casey diligently typed away, Ashleigh worked endlessly on the project's visual theme. "Casey, you know we make a great team!" Ashleigh would say occasionally as the two worked. "You are really good I'M just okay I hate typing! I'm the worst artist in the world" quipped Casey. I'm glad your good at what I stink at," giggling.

"Now class, it is Ashleigh and Casey's turn to present their poetry project" spoke Mr Ryan.

# DEAREST CASEY

Casey and Ashleigh deciding ahead of time, began their presentation with Ashleigh reading Casey's poems

Ashleigh:

"Hello class. It is an honor and pleasure for Casey and I to share our poetry project with you today. The first poem we will share is a Haiku written by Casey called SOCCER RULES:

> SOCCER IS THE BEST RUNNING, SHOOTING,
> SCORING GOALS RIGHT ON, SOCCER RULES!

"Now I will share Casey's biography poem entitled ASHLEIGH:"

> CUTE, FUN CREATIVE AND ADVENTUROUS
> DAUGHTER OF AIRLINE PILOT AND VETERAN
> LOVER OF BOWLING, SOCCER AND ANIMALS.
> WHO FEELS EXCITED, ENERGETIC AND
> DETERMINED. WHO FEARS SNAKES, SPIDERS,
> AND BIG WAVES WHILE SURFING. WHO WISHES
> TO TRAVEL, PLAY HIGH SCHOOL SOCCER AND
> BE A GOOD FRIEND. RESIDENT OF AN ISLAND
> SUBURB CASEY'S BEST FRIEND!

Casey:

"Hi class, it is an absolute pleasure and honor for Ashleigh and I to share our poems with you today.

# POETRY PROJECT PRESENTATION DAY

The third poem we will share is a Haiku written by Ashleigh entitled JACKSON RULES!

JACKSON IS THE BEST BUTTERSCOTCH DACHSHUND - MY DOG RIGHT ON, JACKSON RULES!

Now I will share Ashleigh's biography poem entitled CASEY:

ATHLETIC, CUTE, SMART AND FUN DAUGHTER OF ORTHOPEDIC SURGEON AND KINDERGARTEN TEACHER. LOVER OF SOCCER, ENGLISH CLASS AND MOVIES. WHO FEELS EXCITED, ENERGETIC AND DETERMINED. WHO FEARS WORMS, TORNADOES AND TAKING PENALTY KICKS. WHO WISHES TO PLAY COLLEGE SOCCER, TRAVEL AND BE A GOOD FRIEND. RESIDENT OF AN ISLAND SUBURB ASHLEIGH'S BEST FRIEND!

Upon completing the presentations of their poems, Casey and Ashleigh said, in unison: "We hope you enjoyed our presentation ladies and gentleman." Instantly the class erupted in enthusiastic clapping and food stomping.

"Now class calm down. I appreciate your plaudits for such a wonderful presentation, but we need to be mindful of the noise level" spoke

# DEAREST CASEY

Mr. Ryan. "Class this presentation is an example of outstanding teamwork! Did you recognize how well Ashleigh and Casey organized their presentation? Girls fantastic job!"

As Casey and Ashleigh ate lunch together after their successful poetry project presentation, Ashleigh asked Casey. "Hey, Casey, would you like to go bowling on Saturday?" "Right on Ashleigh, I'd love to. By the way when am I going to meet your brother and sister?" "This weekend Casey. It is my birthday party Saturday. My brother and sister will be there." Casey relished Ashleigh's bright smile as the two basked in the glow of their triumphant presentation. While with Ashleigh the past few weeks, Casey began to feel the joy of happiness again that is what Casey loved best about her new friend her best friend!

"I'll call you after the game on Friday. Will you be there?" With a huge smile, Ashleigh's response was: "I wouldn't miss it for the world!"

## Chapter 5

# "THE FIRST GAME"

Upon settling the pass from a teammate, Casey pushed the ball gently forward with her left foot. Her first touch set her up for a right footed shot at the edge of the opponent's 18 yard box. Casey's shot barreled in on goal.

"Yah, Casey! You did it!" Great goal, Casey," cheered Ashleigh from the sidelines

Casey's goal tied the score at 1-1 with only minutes left in the game.

Casey had noticed Coach Klein in the bleachers watching the game. Coach Klein was the varsity coach for West High School. Casey liked how Coach Klein would compliment her at the Summer Soccer Camps. Casey knew that Coach Klein always looked to bring up at least one middle school player to the varsity squad, especially if the team had made the playoffs.

## DEAREST CASEY

The loud tweet of the referee's whistle indicated a foul. Casey's teammate was clearly tripped inside the opponent's 18 yard box. With seconds remaining in the game, Casey's heart pounded as she heard Mr. Ryan's instructions from the sidelines:

"Case, take the penalty!" Before preparing for her penalty shot attempt, Casey quickly located her mother for advice. The advice was always a cue as a hand gesture. Okay Mom, what are we going to do? Thought Casey. Casey's Mom held out her left hand and arm out, in a low position, parallel to her waist. That meant for Casey to shoot to the goalie's left side. The low arm position meant shoot low and hard. Casey crouched and squared her shoulders to face the goalie and she purposely stood at the side of the net that she was not shooting toward. Then the referee blew his whistle. Casey's shot raced in on goal and went directly into the lower left corner of the net. That's exactly where you aim Case. Mom is always right. 'Way to go Case!" cheered Ashleigh. Casey could hear other cheers, but Ashleigh's cheering mattered most.

"Girls, that was a great win. I am very proud of you. I think everybody should give a team-clap for Casey winter." Casey loved playing for Mr. Ryan.

## "THE FIRST GAME"

He was so calm and confident during the team's games. Even if the game was looking bad for the team, he would always be optimistic.

Casey heading into the locker room with her teammates after the win, was approached by Coach Klein. "Hi Casey, I am Coach Klein. I am sure we know each other. I remember you from the Summer Camps the last few years. I am going to keep this short and straight to the point. Would you be interested in playing on the Varsity team? You see Casey, we made the playoffs, but Jasmine Walters, our starting center midfielder is hurt. She sprained her ankle in practice yesterday."

Casey was in disbelief during the entire meeting with Coach Klein. She simply stood and smiled at Coach Klein. This was something Casey always daydreamed about since she was little.

"Casey, would you like to play varsity? Now Casey, before giving me your answer, I can't make any promises about playing time. However, you can learn our routine and what it takes to be a varsity player for West High School." Coach Klein, smiling, asked Casey, "Casey what do you think?" Casey felt a rush of excitement rush through her body. "Yes, Coach Klein, I would love to play on varsity." "Great Casey, I will speak with Mr. Ryan.

He was hoping I would get a chance to see you play. He has been telling me about you for two years. "Coach Ryan and I will arrange for transportation to get you to the high school. When you get to the high school, I will have a locker buddy for you. A locker buddy is a teammate that you will share a locker with. Casey, it is not the two goals that I really liked about your performance today. What stood out to me was how well you distributed the ball to you teammates. You are an unselfish player, and unselfish players make their teammates better players. Casey, where did you learn to play so well?" "My mother taught me. She played college soccer. She was really good, but she got hurt in her senior year," was Casey's response to Coach Klein's inquiry. "Casey, you are fortunate to have a mother that is so knowledgeable about the game. It definitely has affected your ability as a player. Okay Casey, I will see you tomorrow," were Coach Klein's final words.

## Chapter 6

# "CASEY'S FIRST VARSITY PRACTICE"

"Casey this is your locker buddy, Jess." instructed Coach Klein.

"Hi Casey, it is a pleasure to meet you," responded Casey's new teammate. "Follow me," the tiny girl said. For some reason Casey felt as though Jess looked familiar, like they had already met before. "Casey, here is your uniform. Coach Klein got it ready for you for me to give to you. You will see that Coach Klein is very organized. Casey, this is our locker." We have to take out the ice chest. That's our equipment responsibility. I took the top part of the locker because I didn't have a locker buddy until today. Would you like the top?" Jess politely offered. "No Jess, I am fine with the bottom, responded Casey. Casey curiously scanned Jess' pictures. The first picture was of David Beckham. Casey liked David Beckham too. The other picture was of Mia Hamm. Casey too loved Mia Hamm. Last, Casey observed a tiny picture of a little girl holding a butterscotch colored dachshund. After gazing at the picture for a few seconds, a moment of clarity came over Casey. "Jess, Ashleigh is your sister!" "Yes, Ashleigh is my little sister. She is really cute, isn't she?" responded Jess. "I love Ashleigh. She is in my English class. She is so much fun. She is my best friend," Casey excitedly responded. "Oh, you are the girl that Ashleigh has been talking about. She calls you her best friend too. I am so glad Ashleigh likes New York so much. In Seattle she had trouble making friends. As you know, Casey, Ashleigh is very small for her age. It is hard on her. She tried so hard in Seattle to make friends, but it did not seem to happen. She just love New York because of you," Jess excitedly spoke to Casey.

"Girls enough with the chatter. We need to get prepared for the playoffs. I would like to introduce Casey winter. She will be on our team for the playoffs," Coach Klein assertively addressed the team. The girls all politely clapped and welcomed Casey to the team. Casey was excited, happy and at least momentarily, free of the depression her mother's illness caused her.

## "CASEY'S FIRST VARSITY PRACTICE"

Casey could see the resemblance in Jess and Ashleigh. Jess had Ashleigh's bright blue eyes and blonde hair. The only difference between the sisters was that Jess did not have braces and was a few inches taller. The other difference, which made Casey sad, was that Jess played soccer. She was big enough and did not get hurt so often. Casey knew that must break poor little Ashleigh's heart to see her sister play soccer. She will grow and play like Jess, Casey thought to herself.

As Jess and Casey walked down the hallway leading out to the soccer field, a tall boy called out to Jess. "Jess did you need a ride home after practice?" Jess replied, I got a ride today Jamie." Casey never felt what she felt at that very moment. The boy stood over 6 feet tall and had dirty blonde hair and bright blue eyes. Casey, for the first time, felt jealousy. Wow, Jess has a cute boyfriend, Casey thought to herself.

## Chapter 7

# "ASHLEIGH'S BIRTHDAY"

Ashleigh called Casey seemingly avoiding talking about Jess told Casey "I will pick you up at eleven o'clock for my party. Casey instinctively knew that Ashleigh did not want to lose her best friend to her sister. Anyway, Casey knew that nobody could replace Ashleigh as her best friend. That adorable smile and personality, if it wasn't for Ashleigh Casey knew that her life would be filled with despair. Ashleigh had a way of understanding Casey.

"Casey, just let the horse smell your hand first. Horses need to smell the person riding them first. It calms them down."

Ashleigh was right. Casey let the horse smell her hand and arm first, and then the horse calmed down and let Casey mount without a struggle.

"Casey, just put your hand under your chin. Then you can tell how many syllables are in a word."

Ashleigh was right. Casey used her hand to help her write the Haiku for their poetry project.

"Casey, I should read your poems and you should read my poems. That will show teamwork."

Ashleigh was right. Mr. Ryan complimented about their teamwork in front of the class.

"Casey aim for the head pin. Casey's first turn at the bowling party was a strike.

Casey smiled as she watched Ashleigh bowl. Ashleigh would hold the ball up high near her chin. Then she would begin by heading really low at her hips. Then she would tiptoe toward the foul line. Then she would roll the ball ever so elegantly toward the pins. Ashleigh's ball had a slight curve that would break out the very last second. The ball would usually hit the head pin. Then Ashleigh would let out, in her adorable squeaky voice, "Yay!"

In the middle of Ashleigh's bowling party, Jess arrived, but she was not alone, She was with what Casey thought was Jess' boyfriend. "Casey, I know you and Jess know each other from soccer, but this is my older brother, Jamie." Casey's jaw dropped; she was stunned; she was excited.

# "ASHLEIGH'S BIRTHDAY"

"Hi Casey, Ashleigh and Jess told me so much about you. I'm glad to finally meet you."

Casey, for the first time in her life, could not seem to speak. She could not believe that Jamie was only Jess' brother. She never had a boyfriend or better yet even liked a boy. All the middle school boys were annoying to Casey. She had a crush on a soccer counselor at camp once, but the boy was three years older. "It's a pleasure to meet you too Jamie. It's great having your younger sister's as my friends," Casey responded. Ashleigh, Jess and Jamie giggled, making Casey blush. "What did I say wrong?" "Well, Casey, Ashleigh is my little sister, but Jess and I are twins. Casey could not believe her ears. How could Jamie and Jess be twins? Jamie is so tall. "Casey, Jess and I are fraternal twins." "Oh I see, IM sorry, I did not..." "Don't worry Casey, Everybody always thinks I am older than Jess. Jess is older than me. Jess was born twenty-three minutes before me." Casey's quizzical expression changed. Suddenly she felt comfortable talking to Jamie. Casey and Jamie spoke for ten minutes straight.

"Casey your turn!" Ashleigh tugged at her friend's arm. Casey smiled at Ashleigh and approached the line, she could hear Ashleigh quietly saying Remember Casey, just strike! "Way to go Case!"

## Chapter 8

## "THE HIKE"

Upon waking on a Saturday morning, Casey began to prepare for the trip to the city to see her mother. She would usually pack a book, usually what she was reading for English class and a magazine or two. She would put everything in a tiny bag along with her IPod. As Casey finished packing, her father called her from downstairs. "Casey, Ashleigh is on the phone. She wants you to go hiking with her and Jess and Jamie.today" Casey scampered down the stairs. "Dad, I can't go hiking today. I got to..." "Casey go hiking today. It will be good for you. Mommy would want you to be with your new friends, trust me, Sweetie.

The group of friends hiked all morning. As noon approached, they took a turn that led them to a clearing. The vast clearing was lined with huge maple and oak trees. The trees, shedding their foliage before winter set in, created a whirlwind of colors. The group of friends admired the beauty. Nobody spoke, they just stood still watching the reds, oranges and crimson colored leaves blow through the air. Some would hit the hiking path and settle, some would linger elegantly in the air as if suspended by some hidden force of nature.

"Wow, how beautiful! Jess…Jamie, this looks like Seattle. Casey, you are so lucky to have grown up here. I bet you have seen this a million times." Ashleigh excitedly said.

Casey was mesmerized by how colorful the leaves were. She was ashamed to admit that she never truly appreciated how beautiful autumn was in New York. She remembered warming up for soccer games and the smell of the leaves and the brisk air. Sure, she saw the colors, but she never recognized their beauty. "Yes, it is gorgeous, I am very lucky," Casey shyly responded.

As the group circumnavigated the path they were on, the trail forked. They decided to go left. After another thirty minutes of hiking, the friends came upon a picnic area. "Time for lunch." Ashleigh excitedly spoke, "I did not bring lunch" Casey meekly replied. "Don't be silly Casey, My Mom packed lunch for all of us. She knows you love peanut butter and strawberry jelly." Ashleigh gently took out everybody's lunch. Each bag had a name on it; Casey felt good seeing her name on a bag. She really felt like not just Ashleigh's but all the Marino's were her best friends.

Of course, Ashleigh had Jackson with her. The butterscotch colored Dachshund was absolutely adorable. Casey loved how Ashleigh always spoke to Jackson as if he were human. "Jackson, here is your lunch." Ashleigh had a cellophane bag filled with Jackson's dog food. Of course, Jackson only ate the best dog food, never human food. As the group ate their lunches, Casey could not take her eyes off of Jessie. She just loved how he was so much different from his sisters. He did not play soccer. He was tall. Of course, Ashleigh and Jess were beautiful, but Jessie was...

Next, the group decided to walk up another path because the sign indicated that a lake was only 1 mile away. Upon reaching the lake, the friends noticed people on paddle boats, scattered throughout the lake.

"Jamie can I rent a paddle boat," Ashleigh asked.
"Sure Ash, but what about Jackson?"
"He can come with us. I brought his life vest."

# DEAREST CASEY

Sure enough, Ashleigh pulled out a life vest made for tiny dog breeds like Jackson. "Jackson, give me your paw," Ashleigh spoke. The tiny dog simply sat down and let out a staccato bark. "Now let's go," Ashleigh spoke. Then Jamie said, "Ashleigh, here is ten dollars. Why don't you, Jess and Casey go? I'll wait here. Dad only gave me..." "I'll stay too, Casey blurted out. "I'm tired, I would not mind resting while you two go on the boat, spoke Casey.

As Ashleigh and Jess paddled out to the middle of the lake, Jamie and Casey found a bench to sit on. The two of them watched Ashleigh, Jess and Jackson on the lake.

"Jamie, you are so lucky to have such great sisters. They are great," Casey said. "Yes, they are cool, but Casey you know what...they are lucky to have you as a friend." As Jamie said friend, he gently reached toward Casey's hand. As he reached for her hand, Casey quickly accepted the gesture. She met Jamie halfway and the two held hands for the first time. Casey never held hands with a boy before. She enjoyed it; she felt comfortable. With sudden directness, Jamie spoke: "Casey, I really like you. As a friend, of course, but...more. Casey, acting surprised, responded, "Why Jamie, why do you like me?" "Nobody has ever made my little sister so

## "THE HIKE"

happy. In Seattle, nobody gave her a chance. She was always made fun of because she was so small. She always tried so hard to fit in. Then we moved to New York and Ashleigh met you. She just loves you so much. That's why I like you Casey. You know Jess and I are close being twins and all, but Ashleigh is my baby sister. She almost died at birth because she was premature. My Dad and I prayed all night that little Ashleigh would make it. My Mom was not awake because it was a difficult delivery. Jess just cried her eyes out at home. Then in the middle of the night the doctor called my Dad into the nursery. I thought for sure that little Ashleigh, well, I can't even say it. Then my Dad came into the waiting room with tiny Ashleigh. Jess and I were too young to know what was going on." My Dad loves all of us the same, but he almost lost Ashleigh. That's why he shows extra attention to her."

"So Jamie, do you like me like a friend or..." Before Casey could finish her question, Jamie kissed Casey on her cheek. Casey, stunned and excited, kissed Jamie back, not on his cheek, but on his lips. Casey never kissed a boy before, but this seemed to be the moment. Their kiss, lasting only a second or two ended when Casey asked Jamie if he was coming to the game on Monday.

# DEAREST CASEY

"Jamie, are you coming to see Jess and I on Monday?" Casey readily asked. Jamie responded, "I would not miss it for the world."

Jamie and Casey gazed at Ashleigh and Jessica on the paddle boat. They both chuckled at how much more they could make out that Ashleigh was doing more of the talking. They could tell because the temperature had dropped so that when someone spoke a cloud puff would resonate from their mouth.

As Jamie and Casey laughed about Ashleigh out speaking Jessie, Jackson emerged over the side of the boat. They could see his tiny life preserver and his butterscotch colored coat. Then he must have barked because although they did not her it, a cloud of mist billowed from his tiny mouth. Casey and Jamie, without speaking a word, both thought it to be hilarious. As Jamie and Casey laughed at Jackson's feeble attempt at getting into Jess' and Ashleigh's conversation, Casey and Jamie held hands even tighter.

Casey needed the Marino's. With her mother battling cancer, they were the only thing keeping her happy. They kept her holding on to the belief that, after all of life's tragedies there was still something to hold on to…there was still something to live for…there was something that would get her through her depression.

## Chapter 9

# "CHEROKEE VS. WEST FINALS"

Casey, entering the game for the first time, was excited. She spotted her parents in the bleachers. She could not believe her mother was at the game. Her mother had been very sick the past week.

"Casey, go in for Jasmine. Her ankle seem to be bothering her again. She is limping," Coach Klein instructed Casey.

"Jess, you got me open," shouted Casey. Casey settling the ball with her left foot, chipped a shot just over Cherokee's goalies outstretched hands. The ball went inches under the crossbar and into the net. Casey had just tied the score at 1.

"Yah, Casey, great shot," shouted Ashleigh. Casey's first varsity goal felt good, but she was careful not to celebrate too much. She wanted to avoid appearing overconfident. The goal gave west a 1 to 0 lead with only minutes remaining in the first half.

Cherokee's star forward, Junior Jenna Cruz received a perfect pass from her teammate at the top of West's 18 yard box. Jenna settled the ball and swerved her body to face the goal in one fluid motion. Next, she gently pushed the ball with her left foot and struck a right footed shot. Jenna's shot sailed into the upper right corner of the goal tying the score at 1 before halftime. Lisa Wang, West's goalie, made a solid attempt to stop Jenna's shot, but the shot was too well placed and had too much velocity for her to stop it.

"Don't worry girls, let's set up quick," Coach Klein communicated to the team after the goal. Coach Klein's halftime speech was inspirational. "Girls, you played very well the first half. We need to continue to stay aggressive. One to one; we are in a tie game with the defending champions."

Twenty minutes into the second half Casey spotted Jess Marino wide open down the far right side of the field. Casey drove a low, hard through ball to the space in front of Jess. Jess pulled the ball back with her left foot, sent an arching right footed cross into Cherokee's 18 yard box. Casey, trailing the play, was in perfect position for a

## "CHEROKEE VS. WEST FINALS"

header. Casey leaped high into the air, timing her leap as to meet the ball just as its trajectory began to change direction and began it's decent to the ground. Casey headed down on the ball as she was always taught. Her header, bouncing solidly off the ground in front of the goal, careened off of the inside of the right post and ricocheted across the goal line. Jess Marino was in perfect position for the rebound and she slid into the ball redirecting the ball with her right foot, Jess slid the ball into the net giving West a 2 to 1 lead in the second half.

"Great teamwork Jess and Casey," shouted Coach Klein excitedly from the sidelines.

Casey made brief eye contact with her parents after Jess' goal. She noticed her father in his suit looking as handsome and reserved as ever. He never got too excited at the games. She noticed her mother was holding on to her father. Her Mom needed to hold on to him to stay standing. The Chemotherapy had made her so weak and sick. Casey had a feeling that this may be the last time her mother would see her play. The thought made Casey sad, but she still felt fortunate her mother made it out of the hospital for the big game.

Casey also spotted Ashleigh looking as cute as ever. Her squeaky voice carried every time she cheered. Jamie, standing with Ashleigh, was also cheering the team on, especially for Casey and Jess.

With ten minutes remaining in the game, Cherokee tied the score at 2 to 2 when Jenna Cruz's direct kick from outside the 18 yard box hit the cross bar and into the back of the net.

"All right girls, don't worry," encouraged Coach Klein. "Let's set up quick, make sure you mark up tight, girls," Coach Klein added as time was winding down in the game.

Only three minutes later, Cherokee scored the go ahead goal. Kelsey Peterson, West's center fullback tripped as she was about to hit the ball out of danger. As she tripped, a Cherokee player sprinted to the ball and quickly barreled in on the breakaway. Lisa Wang did everything she could, but the Cherokee player flicked the ball high over Lisa Wang's outstretched hands. The ball went in only inches under the crossbar.

"Girls, we need to push up. Let's go, we need to score!" shouted Coach Klein.

Coach Klein's strategy seemed to work. West's pressure was getting to Cherokee. They were beginning to make mistakes. With under two minutes remaining in the game, Jess Marino was tripped well inside Cherokee's 18 yard box. The referee called for a penalty kick immediately.

"Casey Winter, take the shot," shouted Coach Klein. Casey was stunned." I can't believe he wants me to take the kick. I'm just an eighth grader. Mom, I need your help!

As the referee counted the steps for the shot, Casey spotted her mother. Her mother, using her right hand, indicated to Casey to shoot to the left. Casey nodded to let her other know she received the instructions. Okay Casey, low left, to the goalie's right side, my left.

Casey heard the tweet of the referee's whistle and then she sprinted toward the ball. Casey struck the ball well. It raced in on the goal. It was low, hard and left. It looked good. However it struck with such tremendous velocity, it began to tail a little to the left. Oh no, Casey, don't tell me...

The ball clanked hard off of the inside of the goal post. The collision caused the ball to ricochet across the goal. Cherokee's goalie was able to parry Casey's shot before it crossed the goal line. Casey followed up her shot, but Cherokee's goalie parried the ball out of bounds for a West corner kick. I can't believe I missed! "Casey, great shot!

Don't worry," Coach Klein encouraged. "Casey it was a good shot. You just did not put the ball in the back net."

The referee's whistle ended the game. The Cherokee players celebrated yet another championship. Casey was devastated.

"Girl's listen, you played a great game. They were a little better than us today. Next year we will get another chance," was Coach Klein's final words to the team after the heartbreaking loss.

Casey, you played so well, I am very proud of you," were Mrs. Winter's words to her daughter after the game. "Ashleigh wanted me to ask you if you wanted to go to Friendly's with her, Jess and Jamie tonight, I think it's a good idea," proclaimed Mr. Winter.

At Friendly's the friends never once talked about the game. They only spoke about their plans for the next day. "Guys let's go roller skating," suggested Ashleigh. Jess and Jamie responded, "Right on, Ashleigh." Casey smiled and the last thing on her mind was the loss to Cherokee.

As Casey prepared for bed that night she looked at the picture. She spoke to the picture in her mind. We almost did it Mom. We were so close. We'll do it next year!

## Chapter 10

# "ROLLER SKATING"

Casey loved roller skating. At first she had trouble getting used to it, but Ashleigh was a good teacher.

"Casey, pretend like you are skiing. You need to point your skates in to slow down. If you want to go faster, you need to push your skates outwards, one at a time, of course."

Casey loved how the Marino's had so much fun together. They did not need any fancy vacations to have fun. They would go hiking, horseback riding, bowling the movies, to Friendly's or roller skating and have a blast!

At some point Casey you forgot how to have fun. It was always soccer, soccer camps and vacations to the Caribbean. She loved spending time with her parents on vacation, but it was different with people her own age. Before the Marino's, Casey would go to the Mall with her friends. Sometimes they would spend time in her pool or go to the beach, but nothing as spontaneous as roller skating.

As the day grew to a close, Casey found herself alone with Jamie again. She loved when this would happen. It would not happen often, and she knew she had to make the best of the opportunity. As Ashleigh and Jess were playing a video game, Jamie and Casey sat alone sharing a soda. Casey, spontaneously and out of character, kissed Jamie on the cheek. "Yuck, you got the cooties now," Casey joked. Jamie smiled and kissed Casey on the lips. Although the kiss was brief, it was different from the day at the park during the hike. Casey and Jamie held hands until Ashleigh and Jess came over from the game room. It was not that it was a secret, but Casey and Jamie became content on keeping their feelings to themselves for the time being.

"Hey guys, let's go to Chili's for dinner," squeaked Ashleigh. "Sounds great," Jamie responded.

Casey's happiness made her feel guilty. She felt she should be depressed because of her mother's illness. I'm 13, I need to live and be with my friends. I don't want to be in a hospital all day... Mom is sick, I need to be there. "Hey guys, I'm sorry but I can't. I need to go with my father...

## "ROLLER SKATING"

"That's fine Casey, we understand," Ashleigh quickly responded. Ashleigh was the only one that she had confided in.

"Casey are you ready?" "Yes, Dad." Casey and her father made the arduous drive into the city to spend Saturday night with her Mom. As usual, Casey slipped back into her depression. She never thought of the Marino's or soccer during these drives. She only thought about one thing; Her Mother. Why God, why does Mom have to be so sick? Why now. Why ever? She is never going to see me play soccer ...Was this the end? Was the game yesterday the last time that...?

The thought sent shivers down her spine. Soccer was what made Casey and her mother so close. It was all of her memories of childhood. Her mother was always her coach. Her mother would be the one to dress her for the games and practice when she was little. It was her mother that knew the game, and she always played hard for her. She always wanted to do well to make her mother proud. What will she do if her mother...?

The thought crossed Casey's mind again. Mom is going to die, She is going to...

# Chapter 11

# CASEY AND ASHLEIGH'S SECOND ENGLISH PROJECT

"Now class, your second project of the school year is on the book we have finished. I want you to work with a partner and write a minimum of four poems and create a visual relating to the themes of your poems," Mr. Ryan instructed the class.

"What should the themes of our poems be?" asked Ashleigh. "The themes of your poems should be based on the themes of the book, responded Mr. Ryan.

It made perfect sense. Mr. Ryan's projects were always meant to allow the students to be creative. The lowest grades would usually be in the low 80's. Most projects would be in the 90's. He just wanted to see an honest effort and creativity.

"Creativity, ladies and gentlemen. Be creative. I do not make a million requirements for a reason. Requirements take away from the creative process. I want visuals. Have fun and use your imagination." Casey could see Ashleigh's eyes light up when Mr. Ryan spoke about the visual component. Ashleigh was the artist, not Casey. Casey knew already that she would take the load on word processing the poems, and Ashleigh would spend her time on the project's visual.

"Casey, how about I make a huge white bear? Remember Casey, Cole got mauled by the Spirit Bear while banished on the island. That is when he learned his place in the circle of life. That is when he realized how Peter felt when he assaulted him." "Good idea, Ashleigh. Do you want me to start on the poems tonight, Casey responded. "How about coming over tonight so we can begin?" Ashleigh excitedly asked. "Sure, I'll come over after dinner," was Casey's response.

When Casey arrived at the Marino's, Ashleigh was well on the way to completing the visual. She had what seemed like hundreds of cotton balls strewn on her bedroom floor. "Casey, to make the Spirit Bear look real, I think cotton balls will work," was Ashleigh's first words. Casey laughed and said, "Great Idea."

Casey laid on Ashleigh's bed and began to think of poems for the project.

# CASEY AND ASHLEIGH'S SECOND ENGLISH PROJECT

The first poem was a Haiku:

> Cole Matthews, bully
> He learns to respect nature
> Thank you, Spirit Bear

"Wow that's awesome, Ashleigh responded upon hearing the poem.

Next, Casey figured a bio-poem would be a good idea. It took her about fifteen minutes, but she came up with a cool poem:

> Spirit Bear
>
> Powerful, wild, mystical, beautiful
> Born of the Spirit Bears
> Lover of berries, cold weather, and nature
> Who feels alive, hungry, and strong
> Who fears being provoked, pollution, and poachers!
> Who wishes to eat, to hunt, and be alive
> Resident of Arctic Climate
> White-colored black bear

"Wow Casey, that's amazing! Casey keep going," was Ashleigh's response. You know you have to write at least one poem too," responded

Casey. "I know it, but lets finish the visual first," Ashleigh answered. Casey, meanwhile, came up with another bio-poem:

Cole

Violent, abusive, a troublemaker, sad
Son of abusive father and indifferent mother
Lover of circle justice, Spirit Bear, and changing his way;
Who feels abused, scared, and helpless
Who feels being like his father, jail, and hurting another person
Resident of isolated Arctic Island
Changed person

"Right on, Case, great poem!" said Ashleigh upon reading Casey's second poem. "Now why don't we switch. Remember Mr. Ryan wants teamwork. We both need to contribute on both components of the project"

Casey felt lost working on the visual. Ashleigh was so much more patient at gluing the cotton balls onto the huge cardboard cut out of the Spirit Bear. After about ten monotonous minutes of gluing, Casey got bored. She glued two cotton balls on her cheeks as a joke. "Ashleigh look..." Ashleigh burst out laughing. However, to Casey's dismay, Jamie walked into the room to see Casey with cotton balls glued to her cheeks. He saw the Spirit Bear. "Oh hi Jamie" Casey quickly blushed as Jamie snickered at Casey. Ashleigh could not stop laughing, She laughed so hard that she turned bright red, then purple and then she almost seemed like she was going to faint! That is when it occurred to Casey why she loved the Marino's so much. They helped her deal with her Mom's illness. Throughout all the misery Casey still had the joy of being friends with Ashleigh Jessica, and Jamie. Perhaps is was the only thing allowing Casey to escape her depression.

# Chapter 12

# ASHLEIGH AND CASEY'S PRESENTATION

Ashleigh ambled up to the front of the classroom with the project's visual display. Ashleigh being so short used a chair with Mr Ryan's permission to take the visual to the chalkboard. The class let out a loud "cool!" when Ashleigh moved out of the way of the tremendous Spirit Bear. Ashleigh used thick black licorice for the bear's paws. The hundreds of puffy white cotton balls made for an eye fur coat. However, it was Ashleigh's technique of creating sort of a three dimensional looking head that had the class in awe. Ashleigh, using white a Styrofoam cup had made the bears nose project outward from the flat cut out image.

However, Casey added a bit of creativity to the project by suggesting that they give their Spirit Bear poems to the stringy black licorice claws.

When Casey suggested the idea, Ashleigh grew excited. "Great idea, I didn't think of that."

Mr. Ryan as usual, had a smile from ear to ear watching Ashleigh assemble the visual. He adored all of his students, but Ashleigh seemed to make his day with her creativity and adorable smile.

As planned, Casey would start the presentation by explaining to the class the idea for the visual.

Casey:

"Good afternoon class, it is an absolute pleasure and honor for Ashleigh and I to present our Spirit Bear project with you today.

Ashleigh took the lead on the project's visual. She decided to present the Spirit Bear as a friendly creature, for in the story the Spirit Bear simply protects itself from Cole's anger, hatred, and violent attitude... Next Ashleigh entered the presentation with her charming personality:

Ashleigh:

"Hello ladies and gentleman. As Casey Mentioned, it is an honor to present our project with you today. I took the lead on the project's visual component but Casey thought of gluing our poems to the Spirit Bear's paws. She also helped in gluing the cotton balls to create the Spirit Bear's

## ASHLEIGH AND CASEY'S PRESENTATION

white furry coat. Now I will share Casey's Spirit Bear Poems..."

The class, after hearing Casey and Ashleigh's Spirit Bear poems, let out an enthusiastic round of applause. "Girls," Mr. Ryan spoke, "I would like to speak to you after class."

## Chapter 13

# MR. RYAN'S TALK

"I am very proud of the two of you. This is the second project this school year that you two worked together on. The two of you have a special gift. You know what that gift is," "That we work well together, Mr. Ryan," answered Ashleigh. "Yes, Ashleigh, but there is much more to it. You see girls, the two of you work so well as a team. Now the other students work well together but the two of you are special. It seems that you compliment each other's strengths perfectly. Now as far as the poems the two of you create, they are, well, Beautiful!" Mr. Ryan uncharacteristically enthusiastically said. "Why thank you Mr. Ryan" Casey responded.

"Girls, there is one more project this school year. We will begin discussing it next week. I really think the two of you are going to enjoy it." "What is the project?" squeaked Ashleigh. "It is going to be a film review. You see girls, two classmates must view a film. Of course, the film must be approved by your parents. Then the two students will construct a film review instead of an oral presentation." "That sounds great," Ashleigh responded. "Girls, let me write you a pass to your next class..." "Wait Casey, I would like to speak with you," responded Mr. Ryan as Ashleigh scurried out of the classroom.

"Casey, I really love to see you and Ashleigh get along so well. Casey the two of you are such a great influence on each other. Before you leave, listen try to encourage Ashleigh to try out for the J.V. soccer team. I think she needs a little encouragement. I can tell that it would be a dream come true for her if she were to make it" "I will Mr. Ryan. I am going to help Ashleigh make the team. She is good already. We are going to Coach Klein's camp in July. I think it will help Ashleigh prove that she can play high school soccer."

"Casey, I know this is personal, but how is your mom?" Casey, unprepared for the blunt question, was caught off guard. "Oh she is okay," was Casey's fabricated response. She learned to lie ever since her mother's illness became public knowledge. She knew Mr. Ryan meant well, and

## MR. RYAN'S TALK

that he cared, however, it would be difficult to tell people…No she is not good. Cancer is destroying her body and guess what, she will not live to see me in high school. However, Casey instinctively knew that that response would upset people, so she kept it locked up in her mind.

As Casey prepared for bed that night, she looked in the mirror. She did not like what she saw. She looked depressed and desperate. Why God, why does Mom have to have cancer? Why now? Why couldn't it when I was 20 or 30 years old.? At least then I would have been old enough to contend with the sadness. At least then mom would have seen me graduate high school. She would have seen all of those great games that I will play for Coach Klein. Then turning her attention to the picture, Casey had a flash back of her childhood. "Mommy why didn't you play professional soccer?" Little Casey asked. "You see Casey, I got hurt my senior year of college. I injured my knee and I could not play competitive soccer any longer." "Mommy, did you cry?" "No, Casey, I did not cry. You see, I met your father when I hurt my knee. He was learning to be a doctor at the time. Yes, I was upset at first, but then I met Daddy. When I met Daddy I was the happiest injured soccer player in the world!" "What happened next mommy?"

"Well, Casey, we dated for nearly a year. Then Daddy asked me to marry him. After we got married you came along. You were the cutest baby in the world. When I gave birth to you, the doctor and nurses let me hold you for the first time. You had the brightest green eyes in the world. They lit up the room. Then they had to take you to the nursery. As I lied in the hospital bed recovering, I thought that getting hurt was the greatest blessing I ever received. All I thought about was you. I wanted to hold you again. I wanted you all to myself."

As Casey snapped out of her flashback, she noticed she was not sad. She realized that she made her mother happy. Does Mom know how much I love her, Casey thought to herself. I'm going to make sure she knows before… Again Casey could not finish the thought. Death was not to be talked about. It was "…always Mom's illness," or "Casey, this is just a bump in the road of life," her father would say. He meant well, but Casey could see that Mom's illness had torn Dad's heart into a million little pieces too.

## Chapter 14

# CASEY AND ASHLEIGH GO TO THE MOVIES

Casey and Ashleigh both agreed that they would go see "The Miracle of Friendship" for their film project oral presentation for English class.

"Are you sure girls that it is a PG movie?" responded Mr. Ryan.

We rented Winn Dixie last weekend. We really like the little girl who played the main role. Than we saw the commercial for "The Miracle of Friendship" and realized that she was the same girl, responded Ashleigh.

That Saturday afternoon Mrs. Marino drove the girls to the theatre. They brought a note pad and pens with them to take notes as they watched the film. Girls, I will pick you up at four o'clock. "Don't forget to call when the movie is almost over. I don't wan't the two of you waiting too long for me. Remember girls..." As Mrs. Marino was about to finish her words the girls finished her sentence. "There are crazy people in the world!"

"Casey, don't get any popcorn, we really need to concentrate," spoke Ashleigh as the two entered the snack area. "Well, how about some Sour Patch Kids?" Asked Casey. Ashleigh giggled, she new Casey could not resist Sour Patch Kids. They were her favorite candy, they were her favorite anything except for Friendly's ice cream. Casey bought the largest package of Sour Patch Kids and a diet Sprite. Ashleigh bought an extra box of candy incase they ran out! Casey loved how Ashleigh planned. "We need to stay in the theatre the entire time. This is a major project. We can't buy anymore snacks during the film, and we must avoid bathroom breaks! "Casey, do you need to..." Casey chuckled. "Let's just get our seats. I'm sure we will get enough notes on the film." Casey assured Ashleigh.

As Casey and Ashleigh watched the film they were in awe of the plot. They loved how the boy and girl became such fast friends. It seemed the two characters brought out the best in each other. It reminded Casey of what Mr. Ryan said to her and Ashleigh a week ago. "You know girls, you bring out the best in each other."

In one scene the girl buys the boy a beautiful paint set for his birthday, and he loved it.

"How awesome is this film," whispered Ashleigh. "It is great," responded Casey.

As the film progressed, it became clear that the girl was an amazing writer. Her compositions were so creative and descriptive. It was like her writing and the boys art were one. The two were creative in different ways. Then the boy and girl who were neighbors would play in the woods behind their house. When they played, they would create imaginative worlds. Their imaginations would run wild and come alive in their minds.

"Doesn't this remind you of when we went hiking with Jess and Jamie" whispered Ashleigh? "Yes, it does," responded Casey.

During the movie the unthinkable happened, the little girl died playing in the woods by herself. She was swinging on a rope and the rope snapped and she hit her head. The film did not show it happening, but when the boy returned home from the art museum with his teacher his family broke the news to him. Casey began to cry and ran out of the theatre. She felt as though the film had portrayed her. Ashleigh sprinted after Casey. Casey was crying hysterically in front of the theatre. "Casey, it's just a movie," comforted Ashleigh. "Why, Ashleigh, why did she have to die..That's so stupid. She was only our age. Why, did they make her die?" Casey hysterically ranted. "You see Casey, sometimes tragedy occurs in life and in the movies. She is still alive Case, this was just a movie. She will be in another..." "She's dead Ashleigh." That little girl is dead! Why? Because she decided to play on a rope by herself in the woods. That's stupid!"

"Casey is something else making you this upset." Ashleigh meekly asked. "Yes, I'm sick of death, dying. I'm only fourteen, I do not want to deal with it," shouted Casey.

My grandmother died before we moved to New York from Seattle. You see Casey, I was very sad too. I cried for days. Then at my granny's funeral I realized something." "What, Ashleigh, what did you realize?" "You see Casey, as I sat looking at my grandmother I began to remember all the good times. My granny loved me so much. She called me her little elf. She would pick me up and toss me, she would give me money for snacks. She would say my little Ashleigh you are God's greatest gift to us. Then she would hug me." "So, Ashleigh, how did memories help you?" Asked Casey. Ashleigh pondered Casey's question for a moment. "Casey, you know love never dies, it only grows stronger." Casey thought about Ashleigh's answer for a few seconds. Casey suddenly composed, responded, "Ashleigh you know what, that does make sense."

"Girls, do you want anything to eat," asked Mrs. Marino. "Yeah, I'm starving," Ashleigh answered. "Casey, are you hungry too?" Yes, Mrs. Marino. So how about the three of us go to Friendly's!" right on Mom!" Ashleigh and Casey excitedly responded.

Casey had discovered something the past few years. She alway's had acquaintances that she considered friends, but the Marino's were different. They loved her and she loved them. They cared about her. It happened at the right time in her life. In Casey's greatest moment of need, in her darkest hours, the greatest gift life has to offer, THE MIRACLE OF FRIENDSHIP!

# Chapter 15

# ASHLEIGH AND CASEY'S FILM PRESENTATION

"Hello ladies and gentlemen, Ashleigh and I are excited to share our film review with you today. We decided to create four poems that will hopefully present the themes of the film."

Hello class. As Casey already mentioned, we decided to use the genre of poetry to present our review of the film we saw for this particular project."

Then Casey stepped forward and said, "The name of the film Ashleigh and I saw was called 'THE MIRACLE OF FRIENDSHIP.' It was sad.

Then Ashleigh stepped forward and said, "Yes class, It was quite sad. But it was also extremely inspirational and educational as well."

Casey:

"The name of this poem is FRIENDSHIP NEVER DIES." She is the thirteen year old girl in the film. To provide a brief exposition of her character, she

## DEAREST CASEY

is new to the school. She is cute and athletic. She had trouble making friends at her old school because she was rather unique. In short, she is a fantastic writer. She has an incredible imagination. The teacher loved her writing so much that she asks her to read her composition in front of the class. This poem reflects this fictional character's positive traits.

Although your life was short
You inspired many by your beautiful imagination
Your ability to teach others to dream
Will never be forgotten

Although you are only a fictional character
You will touch the lives of many
Your generosity and thoughtfulness will lead young people
To be thankful to be alive

It is so sad you died so young
You taught young people the beauty of creativity
You inspired us to write this poem about you
We are thankful you exist in our minds

## ASHLEIGH AND CASEY'S FILM PRESENTATION

After Casey finished reading the first poem, Ashleigh stepped forward to read the second poem.

Ashleigh:

"Class, before I read this second poem, I would like to provide a brief exposition on this character's traits. This girl, who was in the eighth grade is a bully. She charges other girls a dollar to use the bathroom. She gets students in trouble, and she picks on the younger students in the school. As the film's plot evolves, this girl changes. She is touched by the young girls kindness as she consoles her in the bathroom. It turns out this girl comes from an abusive home too.

It is so sad you are a victim of an abusive home
You will teach young people that
You inspired us to write this poem about you
We are thankful you exist in our minds

After Ashleigh finished reading the second poem, Casey stepped forward to read the third poem.

Casey:

Although your best friend died so young

# DEAREST CASEY

You will inspire many by your artistic creative talents
Your ability to paint and draw and be a good friend
Will never be forgotten

Although you are only a fictional character
You will touch the lives of so many
Your artistic talents will inspire young people
To pursue their dreams and dare to imagine

It is so sad that your best friend died so young
Your friendship with her will inspire all
You inspired us to write this poem about you
It is a blessing you exist in our minds

After Casey finished reading the third poem, Ashleigh stepped forward to read the final poem.

Ashleigh:

"We decided a Haiku would be a great way to finish our presentation."

A make believe world
To wash away your troubles
A world of your own

# ASHLEIGH AND CASEY'S FILM PRESENTATION

Casey:

Class, Ashleigh and I are pleased to announce the closing of our presentation."

Ashleigh:

It was an honor to share our presentation with you today. We hope you learned as much from our presentation as we did from seeing this film."

"Casey, I would like to speak to you after the class," said Mr. Ryan. Did you speak to Ashleigh about sticking with soccer? It would be a shame if she did not try out for the high school team." "Yes, Mr. Ryan, Ashleigh is going to try out. She is really good. We play all the time in my backyard. She is just so timid because she got hurt so many times last year when she played for her school team in Seattle."

"How is your mother doing, Casey?" The question came as a surprise. Guidance counselors, the school psychologist, people she barely knew would keep asking her how is your mother? Mr. Ryan was different. He really cared The other people cared too I'm sure, but Mr. Ryan, he was special to her. The words came out of Casey's mouth different this time. "My mom's not doing well. She is extremely sick and may not make it through the summer." It was a relief to finally say it out loud.

It felt good.  As she said the words to Mr. Ryan, Casey broke down.  Finally her true emotions surfaced.  Mr. Ryan gently hugged Casey.  "I know how you feel.  My father suffered from cancer also when I was your age.  I am so sorry for what you are going through. Know that I am here for you."

Mr. Ryan walked Casey to Mr. Wang, the school psychologist's office, guarding the crying girl from her classmates.  He held her tight to his side as he scurried down the hall.

## Chapter 16

# "CASEY'S MEETING WITH DR. WANG"

"Hi Casey, my name is Dr. Wang. I am the school psychologist at West Middle School. I am here to help you. What I need from you is for you to be honest with me. I am concerned for your health. Mr. Ryan and I have been communicating about your situation. We know you are going through a difficult time. We need you to communicate your emotions to us here today. Are you comfortable with Mr. Ryan sitting in while we speak?" "Yes, Dr. Wang." Casey responded. " Casey did you know that many people die in freak accidents every day?" "No, what do you mean by a freak accidents?" "You see Casey, somebody's loved one may be driving home from work and tragically they are killed in a car accident. Also many people die at their jobs when tragically something goes wrong. For example, when 9-11 occurred, many workers were killed just doing their job." Dr. Wang, in all due respect, what is your point?" "Casey, the fact that your mother is still alive is a blessing. You need to speak with her as much as you can "Blessing! How is my mom dying of cancer a blessing?" "Casey, it is a blessing because you and your mother have time. In tragedy, as I told you about, people do not have time to say goodbye." Then Mr. Ryan chimed in, "Casey, you know that film that you and Ashleigh saw together?" "Yes, Mr. Ryan." "Well, Case, the little girl dies and the boy never has a chance to say good bye. The boy does not have a chance to say how he felt about her." "Yes, Mr. Ryan, and what is your point?" "Case, time is on your side."

Than Dr. Wang entered back into the conversation. "Casey, you see, you know that time is running out. Mr. Ryan and I are so sorry for your mother's illness. Think of it this way. Take the next few month's to say good bye. Tell your mother how much you love her. Do not let this precious time slip away."

Suddenly Casey found herself calm, the crying ceased. She understood Dr. Wang and Mr. Ryan's message. She had mom for a few more months.

### "CASEY'S MEETING WITH DR. WANG"

Casey, felt better after the discussion with Dr. Wang and Mr. Ryan. She decided to walk home from school alone. She thought to herself that she needed time to make sense of what they told her. They had a point. I have to make the very best of the time I have left with mom.

Crossing the main street, Casey noticed the children of West Elementary School playing. She recalled playing in the very same playground when she was younger. Watching the little boys and girls running around, laughing and smiling, made Casey feel happy.

Walking down the street that led to her house Casey decided to make a sharp right down an adjacent avenue, knowing full well where the avenue led. An unknown force seemed to control her movements. She was heading to the soccer fields she grew up playing on with her mother as the team coach. Arriving at the soccer fields, they were exactly as she remembered them. She headed toward the tiny field where the five year olds played.

"Casey, kick the ball!" Mrs. Winter encouraged her daughter. "Casey, great pass." Then her mother would clap as Casey ran down the field.

# DEAREST CASEY

The memories seemed to drive the depressing clouds from her mind. She felt herself smiling. Feeling blessed to have such great memories of the childhood with her mother. Casey walked toward the larger field where the middle school aged players play their games. It was on this field that Casey scored most of her goals. "Casey, good goal!" Mrs. Winter would cheer, as Casey slid a shot past the goalie. "Casey, you need to get back on defense!" her mother would bellow.

Again, the memories seemed to drive the depressing clouds from her mind. Again Casey felt herself smiling. "We had great times together," Casey thought to herself.

Lastly, Casey found herself walking to the main field. It was the main field where the travel teams played. Casey's mom coached her travel team up to the time of her illness. "Girls, you need to continue to pressure the ball. You need to maintain your intensity. Girls, this game is for the championship." Mrs Winter's words always motivated Casey and her teammates.

Then Casey walked another few blocks past the soccer fields to the church. It was where she and her parents attend Mass on Sunday's. It was where she made her first Communion and confirmation.

## "CASEY'S MEETING WITH DR. WANG"

She often dreamed of her wedding being in this church, but in the dream her mother was always there, smiling and crying. Casey entered the church and sat up close to the alter. The church was dimly lit and there were a few women there praying. "You can go to the bathroom in a few minutes Sweetie," Mrs. Winter's whispered. Casey would ask to go to the bathroom when she felt bored. She never really would have to go! Sitting on the bench, Casey looked up the aisle and recalled walking up to receive her first communion. She remembered her father dressed in his suit with his video camera in tow. Her mother looking as beautiful as ever, smiling and winking at her as she walked up to the alter. She was wearing an emerald colored dress that day Casey recalled.

Gazing up the aisle, Casey saw herself older. She is taller and she is making her confirmation.. She is more confident and mature. She remembered her father dressed in his suit with his video camera focused on his daughter. Her mother looking beautiful as ever. Smiling and winking at her as she confidently strolled up the aisle She was wearing a yellow dress that day, Casey recalled.

Leaving the church Casey found herself walking home. Before entering her house, she stood and gazed at the front yard. She remembered being four or five, and her mother is teaching her how to kick a soccer ball. Casey sees a tiny little girl tripping and falling, but mom encourages her to keep trying. After many tries, little Casey kicks the ball across the front lawn. "Yay Casey, you did it!" Her mother scooped little Casey up and kissed her on the cheek. "My little green eyed angel, you are going to be a great player some day. My little Casey, you are..."

"Casey, where have you been, I have been worried about you, I called the Marino's and even drove up to the school. Why are you so late?" asked Dr. Winter. Casey felt it best to smile and tell the truth. "Sorry Daddy, I decided to walk home from school today." It was the truth, not the entire truth. "Okay Case, just call next time," responded Dr. Winter.

## Chapter 17

# "CASEY AND ASHLEIGH'S BOWLING DATE"

Ashleigh and Casey agreed to be partners in a bowling league for the summer. The league would be June, July and August, every Saturday at noon. Casey loved bowling at Ashleigh's birthday party and when Ashleigh asked Casey, she was thrilled.

Casey had very few plans for the summer. She was going to Coach Klein's Soccer Camp at the high school. Usually going to at least three camps each summer. Casey decided that one camp this year would be enough. Besides she would be spending as much time as possible with her mother. Bowling in a league with Ashleigh would be a great way to spend Saturday afternoon.

Ashleigh's average entering the first week of the league was 152. She even had her own bowling ball!

## DEAREST CASEY

"Ashleigh, what should we say my average is?" asked Casey. "Let's see, you bowled in the 120s and 130s at my birthday party. Why don't we say you have a 130 average. I think that would be a good number." Responded Ashleigh.

In their first match of the league Casey and Ashleigh faced off against two girls from West Elementary School. The pair were fifth graders but they both had 135 averages.

In their first game Ashleigh bowled a 165. Casey carefully listening to Ashleigh's meticulous instructions and advice managed a 133. Their opponents both bowled in the 140s giving Ashleigh and Casey a few pin win in the first game.

In the second game Ashleigh bowled a 150. Casey again listening to Ashleigh's instructions and advice, bowled a 135. Their opponents both bowled in the 150s, tying the match up at one game a piece. However, Casey and Ashleigh's opponents had a few pin lead heading into the third.

As the girl's began the third game, Ashleigh asked Casey, "Are you having fun?" Fun was something Casey always had with Ashleigh, and bowling was no exception. "Yes, I love it. I wish I had bowled before I met you," responded Casey. "Better late then never!" was Ashleigh's response.

### "CASEY AND ASHLEIGH'S BOWLING DATE"

In the final game Casey bowled a 155. She was bowling okay until the final frame. "Casey, why don't you move over one board to your left?" Casey listened to Ashleigh and bowled three straight strikes to end the game. Ashleigh bowled way over her average, finishing with a 165. Their opponents both bowled in the 140s. Casey and Ashleigh won the match by 15 pins.

"Casey do you like Jamie?" Ashleigh squeaked as they waited for their ride. Casey being caught off guard blushed and became embarrassed. "Of course I like Jamie we are all friends." She answered. "That's not what I am asking you, I mean...do you like Jamie in a different way?" Ashleigh asked with sudden directness. Casey pondered the question for a moment. She decided that being honest, although a risk, was the only way to respond to her best friends inquiry. "Yes, I like Jamie . More than I would a friend, but being best friends with all of you is more important. That's why I never told you or Jess." "Casey, don't be silly. You can like Jamie and still be our friends," Ashleigh responded.

"Jamie likes you so much. He told Jess. Jess was not supposed to tell me. He said he wants to ask you to his freshman Semiformal, but he thinks you will say no because of me. If Jamie asks you, I want you to answer with your heart. If you really care about him, then go with him. I don't want you to say no for the wrong reason."

Casey was overwhelmed with all the information Ashleigh told her. Of course she and Jamie had kissed briefly twice. They would also secretly talk on the phone for hours at least once a week. A date would be totally different though. I never went on a date, Casey thought to herself.

The ride home with Ashleigh and Mrs Marino was magical! Casey was in another world. She could not believe Jamie felt the same way about her as she about him.

In her typically personable manner, Mrs. Marino asked: "So girls, how about Friendly's to celebrate your first win of the season?" "Right on Mom" was Ashleigh's response. "What do you say Casey?" asked Ashleigh and Mrs. Marino at the same time. Casey smiled, "Sounds great to me."

That was just like the Marino's. What made their lives so much fun was their willingness to be spontaneous. Casey loved how they did not plan everything out. They simply went with the flow and enjoyed the simple things in life!

## Chapter 18

# "CASEY'S FIRST DATE"

The question came when Casey went over to study for their English final exam on a Sunday. The exam was on the following day. Casey was confident that she and Ashleigh would get "90'" without studying at all. However any chance to go over the Marino's was impossible for Casey to pass up.

The girls studied in the den for two hours. They studied vocabulary, grammar, literary terms and the study sheet Mr. Ryan prepared for the students.

When Ashleigh left to make some microwave popcorn, Casey saw Jess nudging Jamie into the den. "I will keep my little sister busy for a while," Jessica slyly spoke. As she left the room, she winked reassuringly at Casey.

Casey and Jamie never had difficulty making conversation. They spoke for a few minutes when Casey, for the very first time in her life, was asked on a date! "Casey would you like to go to my Semiformal next Friday?" Jamie sheepishly asked. Casey attempting to hold back her enthusiasm as much, responded with "Yes Jamie, I would love to go with you."

"Casey, I think you should wear green to accent your eyes," Mrs. Winter spoke. "Yes Casey, I think your mom is right, however, you are your own person and we want you to decide on your own," Dr. Winter advised. "Green is great!" Casey excitedly responded.

Mrs. Winter was going to be out of the hospital for the last part of June and early July. She was on another experimental medication that seemed to help her strength. She was able to walk again.

"Casey, this means a lot to mom. She is getting a chance to see you grow into a young lady. She is so excited to be home again, and now this...why Casey we are so proud of you. You deserve to be happy. Jamie, well, all the Marino's have really helped you with..." Casey knew the pause well; it meant that the topic of cancer and death was being omitted from the conversation. Casey grew to understand that is was a good tactic. Why talk about what you already know, Casey thought to herself.

## "CASEY'S FIRST DATE"

On the Friday of the date, Mrs. Winter took Casey to the salon to get her hair done. Casey loved how her mother's smile never ceased. "My dearest Casey, you are so beautiful. Your hair color was always so platinum blonde when you were little, now it is such a pretty dirty blonde. You know Casey your hair is...well...caramel colored. That's the color of my daughter's hair, caramel..." "Cool, caramel, I like that for the color of my hair!" She is right, it is sort of like how Ashleigh described Jackson's color as butterscotch.

Next, Casey and her mother picked up the dress. Mr. Winter picked them up and they drove to the store. The dress was an emerald green. When Casey tried it on for the first time, it fit perfectly. When she walked out of the dressing room, her mom cried happy tears. "My goodness, look at those eyes. You got your father's green eyes. That dress makes them so bright. Dr. Winter held his wife's hand. He too was smiling. Always the reserved on in the family. Casey was surprised to see her father holding back tears.

When Jamie arrived to take Casey to the dance, he was wearing a black suit with and emerald green tie. "You look so handsome," complimented Mrs. Winter. Jamie bought Casey a corsage. She felt like a princess in a fairy tale. Everything appeared to be unfolding in slow motion. Her mother's happiness is all that mattered to Casey. She deserves to be happy. She deserves to see me happy. She deserves to see Dad happy, Casey thought to herself.

After a few pictures, Casey and Jamie went to the dance. As they ate dinner, the two talked effortlessly. Jamie always asked Casey about herself. He never spoke about himself unless Casey asked him questions.

After dinner, Casey and Jamie slow danced. Jamie was barely taller than Casey. Of course, Casey was wearing high healed shoes, but she never realized how much she had grown since last September.

As the Semiformal drew to an end, Casey noticed that she and Jamie were holding hands. It was not the first time, but this time it was different. Casey considered Jamie to be her first boyfriend. Jamie felt the same.

The first two times they kissed it was much different. The time on the hike Casey kissed Jamie. The other time Jamie kissed Casey. When the moment occurred and the two were alone, they kissed for the third time. Making eye contact, the

## "CASEY'S FIRST DATE"

two both leaned toward one another at the same moment.

As Casey prepared for bed, she looked into the mirror. She smiled. Then she looked at the picture of she and her mother. The picture, as of late, made her sad. That beautiful woman was dying. Why, Casey thought to herself. The million little pieces were now a thousand little pieces. Her date with Jamie, and the happiness it brought her mother had repaired some of the damage.

There is a lot more work to do, Casey thought to herself. The deep depression still remained. However, it seemed a little easier to bare.

## Chapter 19

# "ACADEMIC AWARD CEREMONY"

"Ladies and gentleman, To present the winner of the Academic Award for the eighth grade English class, I would like to present Mr. Ryan," addressed Principal Smith.

Deciding the winner of the Academic Award for English this year was quite difficult. To resolve the dilemma we are awarding two students with the honor. The winner of this years English Award is Ashleigh Marino and Casey Winter.

"Yah Casey, we did it!" Ashleigh said as she grabbed Casey's hand leading her up to receive the award. Casey was stunned. She had always been a B, B+ student, but never excelled in school, especially English. Casey told her parent's not to come because she thought she would not win an award, but her parents insisted. Again, Casey thought of her mother again. She is probably so happy now, thought Casey.

When Casey and Ashleigh arrived to the front of the auditorium to receive their awards, Mr. Ryan spoke:

"Ladies and gentleman, these two young women worked so well as a team this School year. They created beautiful visual displays, exquisite poetry and exhibited a level of creativity only teamwork can produce."

Casey and Ashleigh simply smiled their adorable smiles, as the two clutched hands.

As Casey and Ashleigh went to find their parents, they discovered the group sitting together. Casey, for the first time, realized that her parents never formally met the Marino's. "Girls to celebrate your achievement we are going out to dinner," Mr. Marino spoke. "Yes, girls, where would you like to go?" asked Mrs. Winter. Casey and Ashleigh looked at each other and smiled. In unison: "Chilies!"

As the four parents talked, Casey and Ashleigh soaked in their victory. They talked about all the projects they did together. They talked about how Mr. Ryan was going to make sure they were in the same freshman class together. They talked about

## "ACADEMIC AWARD CEREMONY"

bowling, and how they were going to win the summer league.

Then suddenly Mrs. Marino spoke to Casey and Ashleigh. "Casey, you know how Ashleigh coaches you in bowling?" "Yes," responded Casey. "Well, maybe you can coach Ashleigh in soccer. She is going to try out for the J.V. in August." "Great, Ashleigh!" Casey responded, "I would love to get her ready for tryouts." "That will be fantastic," spoke Mrs. Marino. "Jess is lazy in the summer, she likes to sit by the pool and talk on the phone. She loves her sister very much, but doesn't have the patience to practice with her sister, and you two, like Mr. Ryan said, work so well together. I think this wood be a good idea!" Casey smiling at her best friend said: Ashleigh, I promise you I will have you ready for tryouts in August. I can guarantee you…" chuckled Casey

As the two families prepared to leave the restaurant after a large pleasant dinner, the servers began singing "Happy Birthday." Casey thought to herself, my birthday is in a week. My birthday is July 9. "Happy Birthday to Casey, Happy Birthday to you. Happy Birthday Casey, Happy Birthday to you!" Again, Casey felt a joy come over her. Happiness was a tremendous feeling that had seemed to enter Casey's world when the Marino's were around. "It was Ashleigh's idea, spoke Mrs. Marino. "Yeah, Casey, it is your birthday soon. You will be..."Casey finished Ashleigh's sentence, "Fifteen, I will be fifteen next week!" "Yes, then we will celebrate it again!" added Mrs. Winter.

Casey thought, What a night! First the award, then dinner then the birthday surprise. Casey again recalled her mother's joy all night. Thank God for this new medication. It has given us some extra time, more beautiful MEMORIES.....The last word resonated in Casey's mind, MEMORIES..... BEAUTIFUL MEMORIES!

Looking in the mirror, Casey peered at her image. A few hundred pieces, Casey. You still have a few hundred pieces left to put back together. Looking at the picture of she and her mother, Casey grew depressed again. Why, why can't these great times continue for another 50 years, 60 years, FOREVER!

## Chapter 20

# "SOCCER CAMP"

As usual, Jess excelled at all the speed drills. She was always a step or two faster than all the girls. Casey excelled at the shooting drills and ball control drills. However, Ashleigh was not too far behind. Although still tiny compared to the high school girls, she had grown an inch since June. She even took the ball away from Jess during a scrimmage. After getting the ball from her sister, Ashleigh did a nifty triple step that Casey had taught her during one of their sessions.

After the step overs, Ashleigh delivered a perfect pass to Casey. Casey flicked Ashleigh's pass over goalie Lisa Wang's outstretched hands for a goal. "Good teamwork, shouted Coach Klein. Casey could see Ashleigh's confidence grow as the week of camp progressed. "Girls, I never met a good juggler who was not a good soccer player," commented Coach Klein. At the end of every camp session, the girls would have a juggling competition. It seemed that Ashleigh, being so compact and close to the ground, had a knack for juggling. She made the finals on the first day of the tryouts. Jasmine juggled the ball nearly one hundred times. Jess and Casey both went out at about 60. However, Ashleigh finished a strong third with fifty juggles.

Coach Klein seemed to take an interest in Ashleigh as camp progressed. Coach Klein thought she was a strong player, even though she was very tiny. It would take a lot for Ashleigh to overcome her size, but she sure was doing a great job of it!

During a penalty shooting contest, Ashleigh again made the finals. Casey had worked on penalties with Ashleigh. "Ashleigh, pick a side. After you pick a side look to the opposite side." "Why Casey?" "You see, the goalie will think you are shooting to that side." "How should I shoot the ball?" "Ashleigh, for now, use the inside of your foot." "Like a pass." "Yes, like a pass, but pass it very hard." "Where should I aim?" "Aim inside the post, right inside the post."

Ashleigh was a great student. After only an hour or two of practicing, Ashleigh was making 9 out of ten against Jamie. Although Jamie was not a goalie, he was big and athletic. Being competitive, Jamie really tried to stop all of Ashleigh's shots. "Casey, how did you learn to be such a great coach?" asked Ashleigh. "My mother, my Mother played soccer her entire life. She played in college, and was picked to be on the national team, but she got hurt and then...""What is the national team?" "It is a team selected to play in the Olympics and World Cup." "Wow, your Mom must have been good!" "You see Ashleigh, that is how my Mother and Father met. He was an intern, studying to be a doctor when he got my mother as a patient."

Ashleigh smiled and spoke:

"The rest is History!"

Ashleigh used the technique in the camp contest. It worked so well that it led her to the finals. In the finals were Casey, Jasmine, Jess and Ashleigh.

After ten shots, Jasmine was the first to miss. Her shot hit off of the cross bar and ricocheted out of bounds. Jasmine, being a great sport, did not mind. She loved how Ashleigh competed and often would say, "Casey, don't teach Ashleigh too much!, She may take our starting job!" Then she would wink at Ashleigh. Jasmine was West's best player. She had a tremendous attitude and work ethic. Most importantly, she is a great teammate.

"Girls, take Jasmine for example. She is always the first player to pick up the team. She is always the first player to say, Forget about it, we'll get back in the game.. You see girls, it is more than grades that get you a scholarship. It is character. it is spirit, it is integrity, it is desire. Of course, talent too."

Coach Klein's speeches always motivate the girls.. It was always positive. "Optimism girls, Soccer is about being optimistic. Negativity will get you nowhere in life or on the Soccer Field.

Ashleigh walked up to the spot, then Coach Klein blew the whistle. Her shot, as Casey taught her, went right inside the post. It worked every time for Ashleigh. She would put enough pace on the shot that the goalie could not parry it. "Ashleigh, you won today's competition. Everybody a round of applause for Ashleigh Marino." Commanded Coach Klein.

On the final day of camp, Coach Klein approached Casey and Jessica. "Girls, Ashleigh is looking good. Varsity, not yet, but definitely J.V. and maybe Varsity next year. Girls, I really like what's going on here...I like the chemistry...I like how Ashleigh is facing off your optimism," Coach Klein said.

### - THIRTY MINUTES LATER -

Casey, looking upfield, spotted Jessica wide open in her right position.

# "SOCCER CAMP"

Jessica, settling the ball, heard her little sister shout, "Jess, you got me trailing."

Jessica delivered a perfect pass to Ashleigh. As Ashleigh approached the ball, Lisa Wang charged out from her goal-keeping position.

Ashleigh, sensing time was running out kicked the ball over the charging Lisa Wang. The ball went into the goal. However, Lisa caught Ashleigh's right skating foot as she dove for the ball. Ashleigh, being so tiny, was elevated in the air over Lisa Wang. Ashleigh seemed suspended in the air forever.....

# Chapter 21

## THE REMATCH - WEST VERSUS CHEROKEE'S

Jessica Marino used the outside of her left foot to push the ball in towards the middle of the field from her far right position. The change of direction caused the Cherokee players pursuing her to sprint past the ball and momentarily out of position. The change of direction gave her just enough time and open field to deliver a pass to an open teammate. Casey recognized Jessica's intentions.

"Jess, you got me open!" Quickly glancing up in the direction of the voice, Jessica sought out Casey's exact location. Then she delivered an accurate pass with her left foot, perfectly leading the ball in front of her teammate. Casey, in what appeared to be one fluid motion, controlled the pass and swiveled her body to face the opponent's goal. Pushing the ball forward with her left foot, she set herself up for a clear right-footed shot. She struck the ball soundly. It barreled in on the opponent's goal and ricocheted off the cross bar and landed in the back of the net. Cherokee's goalie, Laura Smith made a valiant effort to parry the ball but was unsuccessful. Carrying tremendous velocity and accuracy, the shot was impossible to save. Casey knew that scoring on Laura Smith was a big deal. Short, only 5 foot 3 inches tall not only a varsity starter for Cherokee but was an all-league selection. Casey knew the spunky little goalie well from summer league and respected her skills.

Although happy to score the opening goal, in her thoughts Casey still knew her team had a long way to go. Early, it's still real early in the game yet. She could not yet celebrate her goal; could not forget what happened in last year's game against Cherokee. They had taken her glory away once before; they had broken her teams dream of a county championship a year ago, and there was no feeling of content quite yet for her. Cherokee would strike back; they were just too good to be beaten easily.

Just a few minutes after scoring the goal, Casey glanced up the right side of the field. Jessica Marino was wide open! "Case, you got me open!" In response to the voice, she drove a diagonal

## THE REMATCH - WEST VERSUS CHEROKEE'S

through-ball into the open field in front of her teammate. Casey's through-ball was driven to the opponent's right corner flag from her center midfield position. Jessica sprinted to the ball, settled it, controlled it, and then crossed it directly in front of the opponent's eighteen-yard box. Jasmine Walters, playing center forward, was in perfect position to control the cross. After she settled the ball, Kelsey Peterson made her intentions known to Jasmine. "Jasmine, you got me on an overlap." Without hesitation, Jasmine slid a pass directly into Kelsey's run. Kelsey did a fake shot, drawing both the goalie and defenders briefly off-balance. She then took a hard low shot at the very edge of the eighteen yard box. The ball appeared to be heading for the inside of the right post. Laura Smith slightly out of position as a result of Kelsey's fake shot, was unable to get a deflection on the ball.

"Great job, girls - Kelsey, excellent finish!" cheered Coach Klein from the sidelines after the ball found the back of the net, giving West a 2 - 0 lead. Kelsey, the team's all-league center fullback, was great at pushing forward at the right moments in games. Although she made Coach Klein nervous with her aggressive runs, six goals in one season from a defensive player seemed will worth the risk.

After Kelsey's goal. Casey thought it was a bizarre feeling, leading the mighty Cherokee Lady Warriors 2 - 0 so early in the game. *Wow, I can't believe we are up by two goals so early.*

Minutes after the second goal, Casey made a costly mistake. When it occurred, she grew frustrated at herself. *Stupid, Case...Just plain dumb!!* Cherokee's star forward, Jenna Cruz, intercepted Casey's week pass back to sweeper Erin Murray. Accelerating with the ball, Jenna came bearing in toward the goal. As a result of Casey's costly mental error, the West defenders were caught flat - footed. Jenna found herself on a one on one with the goalie. Being creative, Jenna did not strike her shot hard as anticipated. Instead she delicately flicked the ball past Lisa Wang's outstretched hands. The shot traveled into the upper left corner of the goal, just under the crossbar, making the score 2 - 1, capitalizing on Casey's mistake, Cherokee was right back in the game.

Shortly after the goal, Casey speed dribbling near midfield again spotted Jessica Marino wide open down the right sideline. "Case, you got me!" shouted Jessica to her teammate. Without hesitation, Casey drove a long, looping pass to Jessica and then continued to diligently trail the play, anticipating a possible overlap opportunity. Jessica settled the ball and continue to pull it back with the bottom of her left foot. This maneuver set her up for a clear right-footed pass or cross. Jessica decided to pass the ball. She sent a low, crisp, right-footed diagonal pass to Jasmine Walters. Jasmine was wide at the top of the eighteen yard box. "Jasmine, you got me trailing!" Upon hearing her teammate's voice, she knew Casey was planning to overlap her, so she decided to execute a no-look back heel pass intended for her teammate. It worked! Jasmines's pass trickled directly into Casey's run.

Coach Klein was never a fan of these types of passes but never completely discouraged the technique. Often successful with this year's talented team, Coach Klein grew increasingly tolerant of the tactic. "Girls, you know I'm not a big fan of the no-look heel pass. You'd better be sure it continues to work for us."

On Casey's way to the ball, she lowered her level, preparing for a one-time shot. Jasmine quickly moved out of Casey's path to allow a clear shot opportunity. Casey struck the ball soundly with the top of her right foot, following completely through the ball with her entire body. She hit the ball so that it had no spin or rotation whatsoever, causing the ball to wobble like a knuckleball thrown by a baseball pitcher. Leaping to her right, Laura Smith was unable to get a piece of the shot. The ball found the back of the net, giving West a 3-1 lead with only minutes remaining in the first half. "Jasmine and Jess way to pass the ball, great finish Case!" cheered Coach Klein.

In her thoughts after the goal, Casey felt a strong sense of redemption for her costly mistake just a few minutes earlier. *OK Case, this makes up for giving Jenna that easy goal before, No more mental errors Case!!*

Cherokee mounted a dangerous attack with only seconds remaining in the first half. Jenna Cruz dispossessed the ball from Kelsey Peterson at the top of West's eighteen yard box. Executing a brilliant triple step-over. She left the West defenders frozen, flat footed in their tracks. With the West defenders off balance, she used the outside of her right foot to push the ball past them. As a result of her outstanding ball control, Jenna had successfully set up a clear right footed shot. Jenna rifled a shot on goal! Fortunately for West, it deflected

## THE REMATCH - WEST VERSUS CHEROKEE'S

off the inside of the left post. Lisa Wang miraculously pounced on the ball as it was about to cross the goal line. The team was excited after the critical save. "Big save, Lisa! Way to go!" When Lisa punted the ball, the referee blew his whistle, ending the first half. Heading into halftime, the score was West 3, Cherokee 1. Nearly making the score 3-2, Cherokee clearly created momentum they could build upon heading into the half.

"We need to continue pressuring the ball. Do not allow them time to accelerate into space and create scoring opportunities. Why did Jenna Cruz just nearly score before the half? We gave her way too much space! Do not grow complacent - remember how they came back on us in last year's final. Girls, remember, I believe in you, but you also need to believe in yourselves! I want you to finish what we started way back in August during preseason–let's walk off this field as county champion!"

Coach Klein's halftime speech was effective. The team could sense his belief that they truly were the better team.

Although leading 3 - 1, Casey knew that it would take every ounce of effort and focus to see the team's season-long dream of a county championship fulfilled. She knew Cherokee's dogged determination first hand from last year's heartbreaking defeat. They would not go out easily, not Cherokee, they had too much pride to lose without a fight. Before the second half restart, nervous thoughts raced through her mind. *I wish there wasn't so much time left in the game. Why do they have to be so tough?*

During the initial ten minutes of the second half, it appeared that Cherokee had maintained the momentum they created during the final moments of the first half. Unleashing a torrent of shots, they pummeled Lisa Wang with difficult save opportunities. They were taking shots from every possible angle. It appeared that their second half game plan was to push forward and take more shots. Their added pressure seemed to be working.

As a result of leaping in front of a shot taken by Jenna Cruz, Casey was struck squarely in the mouth. To Casey, it felt as if a billiard ball had hit her in the face! She tasted blood. The world spun in rapid circles. Casey gasped. Her knees buckled and she crumpled to the ground. She clumsily used her hands to cover her bleeding mouth. Her eyes closed shut.

Sensing urgency, the referee blew his whistle to stop the game. When Casey opened her eyes, Coach Klein and the school's athletic trainer were standing over her. With the help of her teammates, she awkwardly stood. Blood from her mouth began to trickle down her chin and neck, forming crimson polka-dots on her white uniform. Fortunately Ms. Ryan, the trainer, was able to contain the bleeding, using gauze from her medical kit. "I'm fine," Casey gurgled. She could taste the distinct, familiar, bitter blood taste in her mouth. Taking a ball to the face at least once per season, she knew the taste all too well.

"Case, we are taking you off for a few minutes. We need to clean you up," Coach Klein gently said to his injured player. Casey reluctantly gave in to Coach Klein's decision and ambled off the field, holding bloody gauze over her mouth. Bracing Casey with their arms, Coach Klein and Ms. Ryan gently guided the injured player to the sidelines.

Ashleigh Marino was quick by Casey's side with a water bottle. "Are you okay, Casey?" Ashleigh's voice squeaked as she showed concern for her friend. Casey just had to smile at the adorable little girl who had become one of her best friends over the past year and a half–along with Jessica–and, of course, Jamie, her first boyfriend.

*All three Marino's,* Casey thought to herself, *it was just awesome having the three of them as friends–best friends!* Casey loved how excited Ashleigh was when she made her long awaited debut as the varsity ball girl. She worked so hard to earn her chance, and Coach Klein decided that the Cherokee game would be the perfect time to reward Ashleigh with her first game as team ball girl! Casey and the other girls on the team all showered Ashleigh with attention when she showed up to the field. She looked adorable with her hair done up in braids and adorned with ribbons. Smiling, with those big round glasses and braces, it was clear that she was so excited to be part of the team. Grinning, Casey assured Ashleigh that she was fine and said, "I'm fine, Ashleigh, Don't worry."

After being attended to by Ms. Ryan, she eagerly reentered the game. *Just like last year's game, bloody uniform and all.* Casey thought it ironic that she had busted her lip open in last year's championship game, too.

Cherokee's second goal came off of a well executed set play. Cherokee was awarded an indirect

## THE REMATCH - WEST VERSUS CHEROKEE'S

penalty kick just outside West's eighteen yard box on the far left side of the field. Their left wing swung in an absolute sublime cross. The player soundly struck the ball with the inside of her right foot, giving the ball a rotation that carried it bending in towards west's goal.

Before the kick, the Cherokee players created a six person vertical wall, lining up on the right side of the eighteen yard box. The very moment the ball was crossed, they all accelerated in perfect unison, making it nearly impossible for the West players to mark them. Who else but Jenna Cruz got her head on the ball? Jenna, an all-state senior, was nearly impossible to contain. The 5 foot 10 inch girl leaped up and, with her body taut, snapped a header straight down to the ground. The ball's trajectory created an acute angle, making Lisa Wang's attempt at a save virtually impossible. The header, bouncing obliquely off the ground, found the back of the net. With the score 3-2, Casey knew that her team was in for a fight.

Minutes after Cherokee's second goal, Casey spotted Jasmine Walters open up the middle of the field. Upon recognition of her position, she chipped a horizontal through-ball to her teammate. Jasmine settled the ball, pulled it back with her left foot, and then sent a low right footed pass to Jessica Marino.  As usual, Jessica was wide right; she was surprisingly unmarked by a defender. Speed dribbling towards the opponent's goal, Jessica looked up and swung in an out swinging right footed cross.  The ball glided in the air across the middle of the eighteen yard box, slightly bending away from the goal.  Casey leaped high in the air and headed the ball, but she knew right away that she didn't get down on it nearly enough. The header hit the cross bar and deflected over the goal and out of play.  The collision noise of ball striking post caused the crowd to react with excitement.  Frustrating thoughts clouded Casey's mind after the miss. *Case, head down on the ball! come on Case, you should have put that in the back of the net..*

    With time winding down in regulation, Casey got the signal from Coach Klein to execute one of her signature flip throw ins. It was a rare occurrence that Coach Klein would give Casey the go ahead to whip one of her acrobatic throw ins into an opponent's eighteen yard box.  During practices Coach would say, "Case, only when we really need it. I don't want other teams thinking we are hot dogs!"

## THE REMATCH - WEST VERSUS CHEROKEE'S

Casey would create so much momentum from her flip that the ball would leave her hands with tremendous velocity, carrying a good twenty- five to thirty-five yards in the air. The difficult part was that it was very hard for her to keep her feet on the ground after releasing the ball.

*Case, don't blow it. Keep those feet on the ground...Okay Case, here you go ...* She back peddled all the way back to the fence surrounding the field. Then she sprinted with the ball gripped firmly in her hands. Casey flipped and catapulted the ball, barely keeping her feet on the ground. The ball whistled across the middle of Cherokee's eighteen yard box. Jasmine Walters, in fantastic position and relatively unmarked, leapt high in the air and headed the ball, which careened off of the cross bar. Pushing forward from sweeper, Erin Murray was in great position to strike the rebound. Erin struck her shot well, but it hit the lower part of the left goal post and shot out in front of the goal. The ball fell at Jessica's feet and she fired in a shot without any hesitation.

She hit the ball solid, but it took a slight deflection off of a Cherokee defender, sending it inches wide right of the goal, giving West a corner kick.

# DEAREST CASEY

"Kelsey Peterson, take the corner!" yelled Coach Klein from the sidelines. As usual, Kelsey swung in one of arching corner kicks. Casey charged in toward the ball timing her leap perfectly. It appeared to be heading for the back of the net. *Okay Case, looks good!* The ball bounced up off the ground directly in front of the six yard box, preventing the goal. Laura Smith sprung across the goal line and caught the ball. Casey was impressed with Laura's save. *Man, She has awesome reflexes,* Casey thought.

With less then two minutes remaining in the game, the unthinkable happens. Erin Murray got called for pulling Jenna Cruz down inside West's eighteen yard box. As Coach Klein would say, it was a fifty-fifty foul," meaning it would be argued either way whether the referee was correct in making the call.

Playing aggressively on defense, Erin had pulled Jenna Cruz down well inside the eighteen yard box. The referee, to his credit, did not hesitate; he blew the whistle and pointed directly to the penalty spot. Casey was sure the lead would be gone after the call was made. *Jenna is going to bury this shot!!*

"Karen, it's all you!" shouted Cherokee's coach. To everyone's surprise the Cherokee coach selected

## THE REMATCH - WEST VERSUS CHEROKEE'S

Karen Schwartz, their all county sweeper to take the kick.  Karen slid the penalty shot neatly into the right side of the goal, inches inside the post. *Okay, maybe Jenna does have a weakness after all, Now why didn't she take the penalty?* As she prepared for the restart, Casey's thoughts turned to Jenna Cruz, and why she wasn't selected for the kick.  Hey, maybe Jenna stinks at penalty shots! This made Casey confident that perhaps, a shoot-out would not be so bad after all.  Regulation ended at 3 - 3. *Overtime again, Just like last year.!*

"Girls, we are the better team.  For us to be successful in overtime, we need to control midfield. (Casey knew that it meant her.)  Remember our strategy; flags–long diagonal through balls to the flags.  This allows our forward to sprint to the ball. Forwards settle the ball-control the ball-and then make your decision.  Are you going to shoot or pass the ball, cross the ball, speed–dribble and challenge their defenders...?

And do not forget to be creative! Don't be predictable as they are.  Girls, what are you going to do?  They are going to continue sending long straight up the middle of the field through balls to Jenna Cruz.  Then Jenna is going to try to carry their offense on her shoulders.  Girls, they are not as creative as we are. They are not as good as we are...Remember, I believe in you...Let's walk off this field in twenty minutes as county champions!"

*He believes in us.* Coach Klein always says that. *Please let's not let him down..* Casey wished she could be as calm and confident as Coach Klein. *I know we're better, but that doesn't mean we're going to win. I would love to win it for Coach Klein— That would be cool!!!*

The girls really seemed to respond well to Coach's spirited overtime speech. The traditional halftime cheer was more enthusiastic then ever:

"West, West, West, West, West–Who is the best? –West–Gooooooooo,West!"

"Friendly's tonight, right, Case?" Jessica clearly asked Casey in a futile attempt to break the incredible tension of the moment. Casey grinned in response. They agreed that after the game the three of them (Casey Jessica, and Jamie) were going to surprise Ashleigh with a trip to Friendly's for ice cream–Ashleigh's favorite. It was going to be their way of celebrating together–the four of them after everything they went through the past few month's. Casey and Jessica promised each other that they would be eating their sundaes as county champions.

## THE REMATCH - WEST VERSUS CHEROKEE'S

West's clearly dominated the first overtime period. West's best opportunity occurred when Jessica sent in a well delivered cross from her wide right position. In using her left foot, she was able to create an in swinging rotation on the ball, sending it bending in towards the opponent's. Jasmine Walter's was in perfect position to receive the cross. Instead of taking time to settle and control the ball, she glanced a backward header on goal. Laura Smith parried the ball with her fists, sending the ball over the goal and out of bounds for a corner kick. Coach Klein's instructions were clear.

"Kelsey Peterson, take the corner!" To the surprise and dismay of the team, Kelsey sent the corner kick way out of bounds. "Kelsey, forget about it–not a big deal–drop back quick!" Coach Klein remained positive as usual. "Girls, remember our goal we set way back in August–county champions–let's go out there and accomplish it...I believe in you."

"Hey Case, Friendly's, right, in about an hour after we win this?" Jessica spoke to Casey as the two friends walked to their positions. "Sounds good, Jess," Casey responded and smiled but her mind was completely focused on the game. *Please God, not another shootout.* Casey nervously reflected on the previous year's shootout loss to Cherokee, as she jogged in place, preparing for the start of the final overtime.

The second overtime was identical to the first, with West's controlling the tempo of the game with accurate, short crisp passes to one another. The passing soon developed an audible cadence, as the sound of the girls settling and passing the ball developed a distinct rhythm. *Man, we are playing awesome!* Casey really started to believe the coach was right, that they were the better team. It appeared that Cherokee's strategy was to play for the shootout. They only had Jenna Cruz playing up front and even she was coming back on defense to help. Casey was not at all surprised by Cherokee's tactics. *Smart strategy, they beat us last year in a shootout. You can't blame them for going into a defensive shell.*

West's best opportunity came with Cherokee defenders. She rarely took more then two or three touches on the ball in a single possession. However, moments before taking on the Cherokee defenders, she reminded herself of her mothers advice: *Case, take the ball on your own and accelerate it into open space. Break the rhythm of the other team. They will never expect a center*

## THE REMATCH - WEST VERSUS CHEROKEE'S

*midfielder to take more than two or three touches on the ball,. They are expecting you to distribute the ball to your forwards, giving them most of the goal scoring chances. Case, at least once or twice in a game take the ball on your own and challenge the other teams defender's–they will never expect it.*

Casey followed her mother's advice, executing a nifty triple step over, alternating each step–over in rapid succession, she made the defenders off balance and flat footed. Clearly caught off guard by Casey's ball control skills, the players resorted to watching and not defending. Sensing her opportunity, she blew past them.

"SHOOT!" shouted Coach Klein. Casey's shot barreled in on the goal. *I can't do any better then this. Darn! Not again!*

Miraculously diving and getting the slightest touch on the shot with her outstretched fingers, Laura Smith sent the ball slightly askew from it's original trajectory, which looked to be (at least from Casey's perspective) the upper left corner of the net.

The ball fell innocently over the cross bar and trickled down the back of the netting. Again, the West players and supporters appeared frustrated by Cherokee's doggedness. Stunned, shocked and frustrated, Casey smacked her hands together in disbelief and blurted out,"SHOOT!"

With an air of confidence, Coach Klein communicated the shootout order to the team. "Kelsey Peterson first, Erin Murray second, Jasmine Walter third, Jessica Marino fourth, and Casey Winter fifth."

*Just like last year, but Mom is not at the game with me, It's different without her watching me.* As the shootout was in progress, Casey became deep in thought. Her thoughts were about her mother. She recalled the distinct sterile smell of the hospital, the mechanical drone and beeping of medical machines, and the tears–the crying. Then she began to think about the final goodbye.

" Casey, Mommy wants to talk to you. She wants to see you one last time..."

"Yes, Dad..."

"*My Dearest Casey.* I love you more than anything on the face of the Earth...My little green eyed angel... *My dearest Casey,* you are God's greatest gift to me. Please, don't let this hold you back..."

I won't Mom, I won't. I promise. I love you, Mom, I Love...

## THE REMATCH - WEST VERSUS CHEROKEE'S

Casey's memory of her final moment with her mother was jarred by Coach Klein's gentle voice.

"Case, your up honey, Case if you make this we win..." *If I make this we win, Jenna Cruz just missed... missed by a mile...I can win it—win it for the team—win it for Dad—win it for Ashleigh—win it for Jess—win it for Jamie—win it for Coach Klein—win it for Mom—Mom—Casey* became focused. *For Mom...She* kept repeating it to herself as she waited, what seemed like an eternity for the referee's directions.

*Okay Case, shoot to Laura's left. That gives me the entire right side of the goal in case I am not all that accurate! Case, remember , follow completely through the ball. If I am going to miss, at least it will not be because I didn't hit the ball hard enough. Case, Low–shoot low, you don't want your shot to go over the goal post. Ouch, that would be embarrassing!*

Conjuring up an image of her mother, she slowly followed the referee to the eighteen yard box. The vision of the portrait of her and her mother in the picture she kept by her bed. Her mother well and happy.The two of them smiling and laughing. They are on the soccer field and Casey is carefully bundled up to protect her from the brisk New

# DEAREST CASEY

York autumn air. Casey could remember the ritual. Before fall soccer practices, her mother would meticulously dress her. Her mother would dress her and hug and kiss her, the loving words, the giggling. Those were great moments.

This was the picture Casey and her father chose to display at the wake. It was their favorite memory of the woman they loved. The portrait was placed behind the casket for all to view. She locked onto the vision and secured it in her mind. The memory seemed to be helping her endure the incredible pressure of the moment.

*Mom, please help me through this shot.* "You can do it, Casey," Ashleigh's voice carried from the sidelines. Casey under extraordinary pressure, was still able to muster up a grin as she made eye contact with Ashleigh, who was sitting Indian style in front of the scorers' table. The referee was standing well off to the side, giving her plenty of space to maneuver. Then it occurred–the scream of the whistle. Casey accelerated toward the ball and struck her shot. The ball went exactly in the direction she had planned. It raced in on goal! It went directly into the back of the net. *Yes, I did it!*

Laura Smith, guessing the correct direction of Casey's shot, did not even come close. The shot

## THE REMATCH - WEST VERSUS CHEROKEE'S

was perfect! It was impossible to save. At first she felt a sensation of relief and then excitement, as she stared at the ball, motionless, nestled ever so neatly in the back corner of the net. *That's exactly where you aimed Case!.*

## Chapter 22

# THE CELEBRATION

Casey could hear Ashleigh cheering. "You did it Casey! Yeah, you did it." Then her teammates charged and swarmed her with affection.

Casey never felt so emotional in her soccer career. She felt happy for the West fans. *They deserve it–they* never gave up on us, even after last year's heartbreaking defeat, they were there, cheering us *on.*

The celebration was great! Casey's favorite part was watching Coach Klein being presented with the championship trophy. She loved watching him pose for pictures with the trophy, smiling. Watching her coach gush with pride, Casey's mind became filled with wonderful thoughts.

She did believe in the team. They weren't just words. She always meant *it—believed it—believed* in the *goal—believed* in the dream. County

Champions! He is the greatest coach. I am so lucky, No, we are so *lucky!!!*

Shy about personal accolades, Casey was relieved when Jenna Cruz and Jasmine Walters shared the game's Most Valuable Player Award. Casey was happy for the two seniors. They deserve it.

As planned, Casey, Jamie, Jessica and Ashleigh went to Friendly's to celebrate. It was cute how Ashleigh had no idea the celebration was in her honor too.

"It is so much fun celebrating the big win together," Ashleigh said to the group.

"We are not just celebrating our win, Ashleigh," said Jessica. "No?", Ashleigh surprisingly responded. "What makes you think we are only here to celebrate Jess and Casey's win?" spoke Jamie.

Then Casey chimed in, "this celebration is for you too Ashleigh. It was your first game as ball girl and you did a great job!"

Ashleigh's quizzical expression changed. At first she blushed, and then a smile from ear-to-ear emerged from her adorable face. "Wow, cool! Thanks guy's."

# THE CELEBRATION

While the group waited for Mr Marino to pick them up in front of Friendly's, Jamie asked Casey what was going through her mind before her kick?

Casey thought to herself for a brief moment and then spoke.

"Wow, I couldn't even begin to tell you!"

## THE END

*SONGS
OF
MYSELF
A COLLECTION OF POEMS BY:
JIM P. BEUTHER*

# DEAREST CASEY

## "Dissident Teenager"

Mother yells across the room, "Take
out the garbage"
The dissident teenager ignores her.
He proceeds to put on his coat and swaggers
toward the door.
He knows it all.  He is seventeen!

Mother lets her shoe fly, acute, with accuracy and
high in velocity.
It hits him square in the back.
He proceeds to walk towards the kitchen
And submissively takes out the garbage.

Songs Of Myself

## "Mom"

Leaves are falling to the ground
Their bright majestic colors transcend beauty
the smell of fall reminds me of childhood
playing in the leaves with my Mom.

Throwing the leaves in the air.
And watching them fall to the ground
In no order or no fashion
Gently gliding peacefully to the ground
Pleasing me and making me smile

My mother also smiling and taking pictures
One after the other
As I glimmer with curiosity
Mad with nature! Mad with life!
Running through the soft pile of leaves and diving

Momentarily disappearing and then emerging
One with nature
Feeling the earth at my fingertips
Oh! what fond memories they are
Playing in the leaves with my Mom!

# DEAREST CASEY

## "The Zoo"

Children frenzy to pet the baby goats
Innocent smiles amazed at life
Parents and grandparents taking pictures and home movies
Infants too young to walk in carriages
Brothers and sisters getting along and having fun.

Baby tugs on Daddy's shirt
And then paws at the baby goat
Grasping to pet; trying so hard
Mother is saying "no" but Dad gives in
He leans over and lets baby pet the goat.

A smile illuminates baby's face
As saliva bubbles out of his mouth
He longs for just one more pet
But it is time to go
The dolphin show is soon to begin!

Songs Of Myself

## "Festival of Colors"

I celebrate life's festival of colors
Bright beyond imagination!
The sun beats down on the world
I stand in wonder

How in the world did I get here?
I can't believe how far I've come
I recollect playing in these same leaves
I did not admire their brilliant colors back then

I guess I was too young
Too innocent to see
Through the thick piles of leaves
And celebrate life's festival of colors!

# DEAREST CASEY

## "Dad"

He is watching a home movie
He is tossing a football with his son
They throw it back and forth
No speech; just laughter and smiling!

He is watching a home movie
He is attempting to read a picture book to his infant daughter
She is giggling and playfully tugging at his beard
Silence, just laughter and smiling

He is watching a home movie
He is playing with his granddaughter
He is gently pushing her on a swing
Silence, just her beautiful; innocent smile

He drifts off to sleep and the tape comes to an end
He is sleeping now; in his bed
Silence, besides the static noise of
the television screen
As the nurse cautiously tiptoes across the room to
turn it off

Songs Of Myself

## "The Waiter"

Sweat pours down my face
I carry my dinners up the long corridors of stairs
I'm careful and precise
Watching my every solitary move; just
doing my job!

An old woman suddenly grabs my arm
"I need a napkin and a glass of water"
Her voice angry with disdain
My tray quivers; but I manage to keep it steady

I reply, "One moment Mam

I'm bringing the dinners to my table"
She yells and says, "What is your
name young man?"
I reply, "Please Mam, I'm just doing my job!"

# DEAREST CASEY

## "Grandma's House"

Grandma gently asks me to be quiet
She tiptoes toward me
She braces me by my little hand and we walk
We go into her room and she says
"Close your eyes!"

I listen and she says, "count to five"
I count with the deepest of concentration
When I'm done, she say's
"Open your eyes, I got a big surprise!"
When I open my eyes

There it is, the biggest candy bar
That I have ever seen in my life
"Don't tell Mommy or Daddy," she says.
I close my eyes again and give Grandma
The biggest hug I could ever supply!

Songs Of Myself

## "Northern Lights"

Northern lights sing and ring
Telling stories of the past and present
Stories of war, love and peace
True stories throughout the ages.

Northern lights sing and ring
Bringing comfort to forgotten souls
Stories of hope, courage and salvation
True stories throughout the ages.

Northern lights sing
Sing to humanity the stories of the ages
Stories of Caesar, Mohammed, Alexander and Christ
Humankind at her beckoning cry

Northern lights ring
The passionate cries of life throughout the ages
Sounds of trumpets, armies earthquakes and turmoil
The world's past shining brightly in the sky

Northern lights, please bring comfort to
humanity teach us to understand your wisdom
Embrace us and forgive us for our sins
And continue to tell us the stories of the ages!

# DEAREST CASEY

## "Silenced Walls"

Sunlight enters silenced walls
Years of neglect pierced by yellow rays
Incandescent light illuminates loves and lives lost
We at one time owned an identity
Now we are just lost and forgotten souls
Encompassed in between these silenced walls.

## "Autumn Air"

The crisp autumn air brings memories
All beautiful to my mind.
Playing in the leaves and riding my bicycle
Speeding through the woods; weaving; no fear!

The zealous cries of friends in my dust
Always first and never last
As the brisk autumn air runs through my veins
Wild with nature! Wild with life!

The spirit of autumn evokes my spirit
I hear the sound of trick or treaters
playing tradition
Doing what grandparents did long ago
With their costumes and innocent smiles

What is that I hear? The blow of a referee's whistle.
There is a football game in the background.
I contemplate.  Should I go or should I stay?
Oh! Life's tough decisions on this
beautiful autumn day.

# ABOUT THE AUTHOR

James (Jim) Beuther was born Tuesday April 4, 1972 at 2:47am in the morning. He passed away on Friday April 6, 2012 sometime during the night in his sleep at his mothers home in Florida while on Spring break from his teaching at West Islip High School, on Long Island, NY. James spent most of his life in West Islip where he attended the same schools that he taught at. After High School he went upstate New York to College at Oneonta, where he received his degrees in Bachelor of Science in English and Education. He received his Masters of Science in Secondary Education from Dowling College on Long Island. He recently was working on his Post Masters Courses at St. Roses. He loved to write stories and poems even as a young child. He would give them to me as presents! Jim's happiest times were in the classroom. Teaching was his absolute passion! He coached the Girls JV Soccer team and seventh and eighth grade Wrestling team at the time of his death. He played soccer from the time he was four year's old.

And Wrestled through middle school up in till his second year of college where he gave it up to concentrate on his studies. He spent most of his free time at my house in Florida. He loved the quiet and serenity, and would talk about retiring here someday. Every summer he would leave for Spain the day after school ended for seven to eight weeks, where he back packed doing the "El Camino" (The Way of St. James) for seven to eight weeks. He claimed it kept him centered and he always came back feeling refreshed and lighter! He would spend the last week at my home in Florida. relaxing at the pool. When all was said and done he just looked forward to getting back to the Classroom.